THE DEVELOPMENT OF IMAGINATION

The spontaneous imaginings of childhood have a unique fascination. They take various forms, including make-believe, the creation of imaginary companions, pretence and day-dreaming. One less common but delightful form of imagining is the spontaneous creation of an imaginary private world, which for a considerable period keeps recurring and thereby tends to become elaborated and systematised.

Such paracosms, as the authors call them, vary widely, according to the age at which they begin, the time for which they continue, and the influence of such factors as gender and family. In this unique study David Cohen, film maker and psychologist, and Stephen MacKeith, retired psychiatrist, have gathered together and explored the material relating to over sixty examples of such private worlds.

The result is a charming study of an imaginative activity that has been part of the childhood of such brilliant and creative minds as Friedrich Nietzsche, Anthony Trollope, Thomas de Quincey, C.S. Lewis and Robert Louis Stevenson.

CONCEPTS IN DEVELOPMENTAL PSYCHOLOGY
Series editor: David Cohen

Also in this series

THE DEVELOPMENT OF PLAY
David Cohen

CONCERN FOR OTHERS
Tom Kitwood

THE DEVELOPMENT OF IMAGINATION

The private worlds of childhood

DAVID COHEN
and
STEPHEN A. MacKEITH

London and New York

First published 1991
by Routledge
11 New Fetter Lane, London EC4P 4EE

Simultaneously published in the USA and Canada
by Routledge
a division of Routledge, Chapman and Hall, Inc.
29 West 35th Street, New York, NY 10001

Reprinted in paperback in 1992

Phototypeset in 10pt Baskerville by
Mews Photosetting, Beckenham, Kent
Printed in Great Britain by Mackays of Chatham PLC

British Library Cataloguing in Publication Data

Cohen, David, *1946–*
The development of imagination : the private worlds of
childhood. (Concepts in developmental psychology.)
1. Children. Paracosms
I. Title – II. MacKeith, Stephen, A., *1906–* III. Series
155.4′13

Library of Congress Cataloging in Publication Data

Cohen, David, 1946–
The development of imagination : the private worlds of childhood /
David Cohen, Stephen A. MacKeith.
p. cm. – (Concepts in developmental psychology)
1. Imagination in children. I. MacKeith, Stephen A., 1906–
II. Title. III. Series.
BF723.I5C63   1990
155.4′133–dc20   90–8329
ISBN 0–415–04636–X   CIP

CONTENTS

Series foreword   vi

Acknowledgements   vii

Introduction   1

1 TOYS   24

2 PARTICULAR PLACES AND LOCAL
   COMMUNITIES   38

3 ISLANDS, COUNTRIES, AND THEIR
   PEOPLES   53

4 SYSTEMS, DOCUMENTS, AND LANGUAGES   70

5 UNSTRUCTURED, SHIFTING, AND IDYLLIC
   WORLDS   96

6 CONCLUSION   102

Appendices   107

Further reading   112

References   115

Index   118

SERIES FOREWORD

Since psychology became a 'scientific' discipline, one of its key areas has been developmental psychology. How children grow up remains one of the most important, and intriguing, of questions. For a long time, outside psychoanalysis, developmental psychology was dominated by studies of intelligence, but children don't just grow cognitively. In the last fifteen years, there have been a wealth of studies on different aspects of growing up – from how children begin to relate, to how they learn to speak, to how their sense of humour matures. Video recording techniques have helped to widen the scope of developmental psychology so it is now possible to observe children more accurately than ever before. The whole area of study is exciting and growing.

This series aims to reflect the growth of developmental psychology. Each volume will be written by an interesting psychologist whose brief is to write an account of a particular developmental patch. For some books that patch will be conventionally defined. Other books will take a wider than usual look at a particular area. Some will take a concept that is well accepted in everyday life, such as conscience, but which academic psychology has tended to ignore or, at best, to treat intellectually. Each book will offer a clear, readable, and authoritative account of the latest ideas and research in the area at a level which is both interesting to the specialist and accessible to the undergraduate.

David Cohen

ACKNOWLEDGEMENTS

Our first tribute clearly must be to the late Robert Silvey, who initiated the study of the spontaneous imaginary private worlds of children, upon which this book is based.

For such worlds, Ben Vincent coined the convenient term 'paracosm'. The late Dr Vladimir Kahan generously assisted the study, especially in the drafting of the questionnaire for respondents. Later on, Jonathan Silvey helped with the calculations. At various stages, Bill MacKeith gave valuable editorial guidance.

Warmest thanks are due to all the paracosmists who completed Robert Silvey's questionnaire. We analysed and drew our main conclusions from the answer-sets of the first 57 of these respondents. It is from those answer-sets that the examples, summarised in the present book, have been selected. The 'names' used are, in fact, pseudonyms, because anonymity was promised to all our respondents.

Stephen A. MacKeith

INTRODUCTION

Human beings love stories. They're more ambivalent about story-tellers. If we say a child lives 'in a world of his own', it isn't usually a compliment. Children don't have to live in the real world as much as adults do but we praise children who are mature, who knuckle down to their maths, or who play sensible games. In general, we give children some leeway and let them get away with day-dreaming. But the licence is only temporary. Come maturity, they'll have to drop the dreaming, grow up, and grow out of it.

The phrase 'in a world of his own' doesn't mean that literally, of course. When we grumble that little Adam or Emily is yet again 'in a world of their own', it tends to mean that they are looking lost, and not paying attention to important adult matters. The phrase suggests a lack rather than anything positive. After complaining that a child is in a world of their own, it would be an odd adult who went on to ask if that world was Fairyland or Ruritania or Teddyworld. But sometimes children do take such trips in their minds. It is well known that children have imaginary companions.

This book is an account of a different kind of imaginary activity – the creation of imaginary worlds. Robert Silvey and Stephen MacKeith, who collected the material, christened these 'paracosms' and were determined that the two things should not be confused. Since this is not meant to be a technical book, we do not always stick to this term but we have set out the most interesting and charming of these creations. Children can slip out of social life without too much fuss. The 8-year-old can leave the table and go and play at the bottom of the garden where the trees become the masts of a pirate ship. Parents often chide a child who day-dreams a great deal but it isn't usually seen as a serious problem. Our response to adults who engage in such

1

wayward behaviour is very different. Often we penalize them; sometimes we worship them. Take one extreme, the vagrant who prefers to drift down the arches, letting himself go, losing work and relationships. Today, that person is likely to get medical help and a social worker even if he doesn't want them. In P.G. Wodehouse's graphic phrase, he becomes 'a candidate for Colney Hatch', Colney Hatch being a lunatic asylum on the edge of London. Psychiatric patients can feel that they are in a world of their own. They start believing they are Napoleon or hear voices and instructions from an assortment of devils, deities, and (given technological progress) television sets. Recent research on schizophrenics suggests that some of them have poor motor control. They are genuinely not skilled at fine motor and perceptual discrimination (*American Journal of Psychiatry*, July 1989). They are poor at controlling the sequences of willed action that most of us take for granted. It's not surprising therefore that they should feel someone else controls them.

If society penalizes the psychiatric patient who is 'in a world of their own', it often rewards the successful professional artist who is a world-weaver. The noun is deliberate because one of the more curious phenomena of modern culture is our addiction to adult literary fantasy worlds. Tolkien, Borges, Castenada, Doris Lessing in her sci-fi writings, Isaac Asimov, and Ursula Le Guin have in common the skill of being creators of new worlds. In many of their works, their self-made worlds matter, and fascinate, more than their characters or plots do. Most of these authors do not have a didactic or satirical purpose as in Utopias of old. They imagine new worlds for, it seems, the sheer delight of the act though, of course, they are sometimes designed as critical commentaries on the present.

Visual artists have also created worlds of their own. In 1977 an extra-ordinary American painter was killed in a fire in Amsterdam. Donald Evans painted only postage stamps. His stamps defined his own universe as they were for imaginary countries, imaginary rulers, and imaginary events. The Swedish painter, Claes Oldenburg, said that he drew on his imaginary childhood world for all of his adult work. Marc Chagall conjured up in his bright surrealism of cows, fiddlers, lovers, and moons a world that was far from logical. So did Klee. These artists all created worlds.

We have, therefore, a paradox. To create a world of one's own may be taken as a sign of genius or of madness. These two poles exist. The 'mad' adult believes, more or less completely, that his or her fantasies are 'real'. However, the child does not.

One of the earliest instances recorded of children making up such a world is that of the four Brontë children. Charlotte and Branwell, Emily and Anne Brontë lived with their widowed father at Haworth parsonage on the edge of the Yorkshire moors. They were educated at home and lived a rather isolated life. When Charlotte was 9 and her three younger siblings 5 to 8, their two older sisters died. The surviving children began to create worlds with Charlotte and Branwell taking the lead.

At first they experimented with a variety of fantasy worlds. In June 1826 their father gave them a set of toy soldiers and this gift sparked into being Verdopolis, the great Glass Town, which later blossomed into the country of Angria. Charlotte and Branwell became completely absorbed in the elaboration of Angria. They introduced into it contemporary characters, politicians, soldiers, and writers. They produced a never-ending stream of relevant miniature writings; there were poems and documents, fables and chronicles. Like magpies, the Brontë children incorporated every scrap of information into their new world. There was an interesting division of labours: Branwell tended to develop the political and military side of Angria while Charlotte concentrated on the personalities and relationships of the chief characters. In time, Anne and Emily created a world of their own, Gondal, leaving Angria to the elder two. Gondal had far less pomp and luxury than Angria but it had deeper feelings. It would be nice to suggest that this difference emerged in the sisters' masterpieces, with Charlotte's *Jane Eyre* being a shade less emotional than Emily's *Wuthering Heights*, but *Jane Eyre* is emotional enough.

It has often been argued that these childhood fantasies indirectly helped the Brontës develop as novelists. Unlike the imaginary worlds of most children, that of the Brontës survived into their adulthood. Anne referred to Gondal in her letters when she was 20 and Emily kept a lively sense of the fabled Gondal till her own death at 30. Angria, in fact, inspired her finest poems. Charlotte planned to give up Verdopolis when she went to boarding school and even wrote a poem about its deliberate destruction; but when she came back from school at 16 she soon went back to her imaginary world.

In her early 20s she wrote five little novels about Angria, but these were never published in her lifetime. When she was 31 she published her major novel, *Jane Eyre*; this book was about the real world and based on events in her real life.

We have no intention of retelling the Brontë story but one quotation from a passage which Charlotte wrote at 20 shows how powerful the grip of Angria was.

Never shall I, Charlotte Brontë, forget how distinctly I, sitting in the school room at Row Head, saw the Duke of Zamorna leaning against the obelisk . . . . I was quite gone. I had really utterly forgot where I was . . . . I felt myself breathing quick and short as I beheld the Duke lifting up his sable crest, which undulated as the plume of a hearse waves to the wind . . . . 'Miss Brontë, what are you thinking about', said a voice, and Miss Lister thrust her little, rough black head into my face.

Charlotte was quite clearly in a world of her own.

In this book we explore the imaginary worlds mainly of ordinary children who have imaginary worlds but who do not usually flower into writers.

IMAGINATION

Psychologists have had an ambivalent attitude to the imagination. On the one hand, it fascinates. Just as no other species can speak, no other species can imagine or invent. On the other hand, it is extremely hard to study imagination – especially experimentally.

The 960-page *Handbook of Developmental Psychology* (Wolman 1982) has no entry indexed under imagination – and nothing under any subject that might be linked with it. The *Oxford Companion to the Mind* (Gregory 1987), which is wonderfully comprehensive, doesn't have an entry under imagination. It has room, however, for Chinese psychology, castration anxiety, and much more than might seem to have no better claim to being 'of the mind'. On the whole, philosophers have been more interested than psychologists. Warnock (1980) in her *Imagination* reviewed the theories of Locke, Berkeley, Hume, Kant, and, more recently, Sartre. Warnock focused on the connection between imagination and perception. Imagination is, she suggested, the 'image-making' facility. It goes beyond the sense data of perception though not necessarily in any coherent way. When psychologists have studied creativity, they have tended to view it slightly differently.

Two broad trends have contributed to the neglect of the imagination as a subject for psychological research. First, experimental psychology has concentrated on sensory processes and on learning. Few things are further from the imagination than questions of how we learn nonsense syllables or lists or exercise motor skills. Second, when creativity has been studied, it's often been in the context of abnormal psychology. Some theorists have argued that art is the by-product either of sexual frustration or of madness. One of the most remarkable examples of that tendency is Eissler's view (1962) that no artist could flourish who didn't suffer from serious sexual problems. Many artistic biographies do tend to dwell on the 'crazy genius' like Van Gogh or Richard Dadd, who was one of the first inmates of Broadmoor, the asylum for criminally insane people. Some authors leave the feeling that Van Gogh would never have painted if he hadn't gone crazy. Such studies of the imagination in adults have perhaps over-stressed this theme.

Furthermore, it is hard to conceive of a *science* of the imagination and, for much of its history, psychology has been concerned to establish its credentials as a science. Some psychologists have actually pursued creative writing. Don Bannister was a polished novelist; Liam Hudson has published poems and a novel; most famously, B.F. Skinner published a Utopian novel, *Walden Two* (1948). But even though these psychologists differed widely in their theoretical views, they were all at pains (certainly in interviews with me) to stress how separate these two aspects of their work were. Fiction was fiction; science was fact. Novel-writing was far away from their normal scientific work. In a sense it's true but their insistence on making the point emphasizes how nervous many psychologists become when dealing with the subject of the imagination. Is it as if it seems impossible that there could be a science of imagination at all?

The entry in the *Oxford Companion to the Mind* that comes closest to imagination is one on creativity. In it Liam Hudson, who reported some powerful experiments on creative school children in the 1960s, argues that creativity has been studied in two different ways – biographically and through what he calls the 'creative school' (Hudson 1987).

The 'creative school' is very much an American product. In the 1930s American psychology began to fret about whether intelligence testing could reveal everything about our ability to think. Large-scale longitudinal projects like Terman's Gifted IQ sample were following subjects through life. Would their IQ affect their fate? It began to dawn on some psychologists that this was a rather narrow approach. Experimentalists like J.P. Guilford (1957) argued that IQ tests posed only one kind of question – questions that had one correct answer.

In life, even as lived in the psychological laboratory, there were more complex issues. Guilford suggested that one should try to examine a different kind of thinking, thinking which tried to cope with problems that didn't have one set solution but a host of possible answers. In real life, and crucially in real management in industry, the options were often more like that. There is no one answer to the questions how many uses are there for a brick or how yellow do you paint?

The move was popular in business circles which in the USA have been interested in psychology since 1910 when Pillsbury wrote his *Industrial Psychology*. American industry wanted creative solutions. In 1920, for example, John B. Watson, the founder of behaviourism, solved the problem of how to sell the brand of coffee he represented by getting retailers to place it by their tills. He invented 'point of sale' sale.

There has been a great deal of work in this tradition. It has had some valuable consequences, including trying to make creativity operational. For example, Getzels and Jackson (1962) argued that it was possible to identify two quite different cognitive styles. Convergers did well at conventional IQ tests because their intellect could converge on the one correct solution. 'Creative' divergers, however, were able to think up and produce endless variations on the use of a brick. At the same time, it was alleged that creativity lay in the ability to make associations between unlikely elements. The Remote Associates Test (RAT) allowed you to discover if you could find a link between Swiss, mouse, and blue. Oh for a Muse of Fire to inspire the answer: cheese!

It is possible to see that this kind of creativity isn't quite what we normally mean by being imaginative. It has been rather doctored to suit the conventions of psychological testing. The RAT probably correlates excellently with the ability to do crosswords. This is not a negligible skill at all but neither is it imagination as we normally understand it. The RAT claims there are improbable but correct solutions. But most imaginative activities don't set out to answer problems. There is no question to which the *Mona Lisa* or *King Lear* is the answer.

In fact, Hudson made his reputation by showing that divergent and convergent thinking didn't really divide creative and non-creative school children. In *Contrary Imaginations* (1966) he showed that divergers tended to be arts specialists while convergers were science specialists. Convergers who did badly on tests, like how many uses are there for a brick – the creative can rattle out fifty uses – still managed to invent computer programs. Real creativity was far more specific than Getzels and Jackson thought. Hudson then moved into rather more abstract areas of interest, perhaps because his discoveries led to a certain impasse. How could he show scientifically what made a particular child creative in a particular situation? It would be a question of biography; and biographical answers remain elusive.

It has been traditional also to try and understand the imagination in general through the life histories of great men and women. Detailed analysis of the Great Lives will yield the clues to creativity. There is no doubt that the lives of geniuses are fascinating and instructive. However, it's hard to construct any very satisfactory simple theory of creativity since geniuses are irritating enough to lead very diverse and individual lives. One study of painters (Wittkower and Wittkower 1963) found that there were celibate painters, happily married painters, utterly unfaithful cad painters, and painters who desperately wanted to make it with women but never managed to do so. The randy Picasso, the respectable Rembrandt, and the repressed Leonardo make it hard to arrive at a simple equation that connects sexuality or libido and artistic achievement.

Freud, who first dabbled in what we now call psychobiography, was respectful of art. He said that it was hard to pin any crude psychodynamic explanation to works of genius. Nevertheless, Freud first suggested that artists need to do art, or to use their imaginations, because they cannot express all their libidinal energy in life. It has been argued that Van Gogh managed to produce such a welter of paintings in his last two years because he gave up all hopes of women or marriage. Nevertheless, the genre is fraught with problems. Any biography has to establish and interpret complex facts. Often crucial private papers are missing. Being sure of what dreams mean, a crucial analytic enterprise, is not at all easy when those dreams occurred centuries ago. There are more banal problems, too. Take Freud's *Leonardo* (1910): Freud argued that Leonardo's repressed libido was crucial to his art. Sexual energy that didn't express itself physically erupted in miraculous paintings. Freud made much of a dream of Leonardo's that concerned the tail of a vulture. It turned out, alas, that Freud misread the Italian and that Leonardo's dream had nothing to do with tails or vultures. Freud's neat psychobiographical piece of detection crumbled in linguistic ruins. This failure needn't invalidate the whole Freudian approach but it illustrates its perils.

Perhaps the most comprehensive attempt to understand the motives of artists is Storr's *Dynamics of Creation* (1972). Storr tried to analyse a number of psychological profiles shared by great scientists and artists. He argued that different artists exhibited different psychopathological traits. Stravinsky, Ibsen, and Rossini were obsessional, for example; others, like Einstein and Newton, were schizoid and used their theories to keep people at bay. In some writers, like Ian Fleming (if the James Bond books are art), the work of art provided the simplest kind of wish fulfilment. Fleming, who couldn't be Bond, made up Bond who cut a dash in the world which Fleming never managed. Some geniuses like Baudelaire were very close to psychotic. Storr argued that, in order to be creative, a person has to have access to his or her inner world and to be able to exercise control over that world. Art is a means to psychological integration. The artist lives in a state of tension created by his or her psychological problems. Storr noted that many artists displayed highly opposed traits of personality. They tended to be psychologically androgynous, being both highly masculine and feminine; the genius lies in the way they use that tension. Instead of collapsing into madness, artists try to control such conflicts through the art. Art isn't so much consolation as a way of control. And the artists may not even know what they are trying to do or manage to achieve.

Storr is a persuasive writer; he argued for some interesting links between some artistic works and the underlying problems of their creators. Here was the dynamic of creation, but there are some problems with this view. There are people who have the same dynamics that Storr identifies but who don't become geniuses. Usually since we're not much interested in those who don't make it into the *Who's Who* of history we know little of them. In his time, Edmund Gosse was thought of as a minor talent who wrote one good book, *Father and Son* (1907). The life of Edmund Gosse had many of the tensions that Storr found in geniuses. Gosse lost his mother young. He lived with an interesting but demanding father who was a gifted geologist but couldn't bear to accept that Darwin was right because it would topple religion. The young Gosse lived with his father's conflicts. From an early age, he helped the old man beachcombing for interesting fossils. Edmund Gosse worked through his own conflicts in writing *Father and Son*. He did what Storr requires of a genius very directly. Yet Gosse isn't much remembered and, in so far as he is, it is just for that one book *Father and Son*. Equal dynamics may not produce equal art.

Less anecdotal studies than Storr's also produce interesting but inconclusive results. Anne Roe, for example, interviewed 64 successful biologists, physicists, and astronomers. Her samples were small but her technique rigorous. She discovered that there were certain biographical similarities between specialists. Physicists tended to have lost their fathers before the age of 11, for example. Most of the scientists scored high. Roe (1953) found whatever their discipline, there were similarities between them. The main one was that all of them tended to be fanatically devoted to their work; they didn't have a concept of leisure. Work never stopped because the puzzles about nature that confronted them never let them alone. Roe's investigation was painstaking and she found some intriguing differences between great biologists and physicists. But it is clear that hard work isn't a very convincing explanation of why some people become so creative scientifically. Analysing the lives of great scientists doesn't produce any general enlightenment. How many researchers work hard and find they asked the right questions?

Simonton (1989) has put forward a new theory of scientific genius, which claims that the personality characteristics of great scientists are only a small part of the equation. A high IQ is, he accepts, vital. So is hard work and a willingness to take individual risks. Simonton notes too that many of the great scientists like Newton, Einstein, and Poincaré were driven to seek harmony and order in nature. Where Storr saw that as in part a schizoid attempt to impose a whole new world, Simonton suggests that it may lead scientists to behave irrationally. They will seek evidence that confirms their view instead of being methodologically well behaved and seeking to falsify their new theories.

Hudson's own view of creativity in the *Oxford Companion of the Mind* offers an interesting example of what Simonton complains of. Hudson (1987) argues that madness and genius aren't linked. But he suggests for example that great artists often do have to pay a price for great works. Hudson argues that the German poet, Rainer Maria Rilke (1875-1926), suffered both depression and a writer's block for ten years after 1914. Then, in an astonishing burst of genius, Rilke wrote a sequence of sixty-four sonnets in eight weeks. Hudson suggests that for Rilke the period of depression and block was crucial. Without its frustrations, there never would have been the exquisite sonnets. Does this mean that for every poet blocks and depression lead to creative flow?

It is very easy to provide two quite different kinds of counter-instances. T.S. Eliot (1888-1965), a poet of the same period, worked

9

consistently at a high standard from *Prufrock* in 1917 to *Murder in the Cathedral* in 1935. There were intervals in which he felt he couldn't write but these were not very long. During them he busied himself with prose. Philip Larkin has in many ways been seen as Eliot's heir. He wrote far less; from 1970 he quietly bemoaned the death of his muse. Poems wouldn't come. He felt, and his *Collected Works* show, that they never came again. He dried up and showed some bitterness. There was never the release that Rilke found in those final poems. The block didn't erupt into creativity. We do not intend to criticize Hudson but merely seek to illustrate the limits and perils of biography.

Imagination is elusive – its development more so. The study that follows isn't an answer to all of the problems but an attempt to contribute some much needed, and unusual, data in the area of developmental psychology.

Developmental psychologists have been aware of these limitations in attempts to study the imagination. With children, the problems are different. Children spend a great deal of their time playing. Some, but not all, play involves imaginative acts. Pretend play in which children act out a variety of often swiftly changing roles is the most obvious form of 'creative play'. In an earlier book (Cohen 1987) I argued that psychologists had tried to pin down the causes of play without too much success. Most assumed play had to have some unifying purpose instead of being useful for many psychological developments – and also being fun. Storr (1972) also looked at the links between creativity and children's play. Techniques of monitoring children's play have improved so that there are now records of long sequences of play (Fein 1984). But in real life, play comes and goes; children drop in and out of roles. Unlike art, nothing remains. Play's magic is partly that it is ephemeral.

This book deals with different and unusual material: the results of games that didn't disappear and weren't meant to. The children whose imaginary worlds are recorded here kept returning to them. Many did more than just remember them; they kept written records of highly structured fantasy worlds. These worlds offered opportunities for play that some children loved. The traditional literature on play leaves such structures for play largely out of account.

Children play in many different ways. They may scamper about in a disorganized fashion. They may organize games which mimic adult pastimes. In 1984, the summer of the Olympic Games, my 9-year-old son organized a long-jumping competition in the back garden in which he and three friends (one as young as 5) made attempts on the world long-jump record. Young children act out all kinds of roles. Reuben spent a long period of time between the ages of 2 and 5 playing Batman and Superman. He assumed these roles by throwing a piece of cloth around himself as a kind of cape. That was all it needed to transform him into a superhero. These episodes of play are interesting because even though they *can* go on a long time, they usually tend to be very transient. Playing a role – say of Superhero and Baddie – two children can while away an afternoon. But nothing remains of their efforts and imagination except, perhaps, their memory of it. You could argue that it's no accident that we call a theatrical performance a play. Once the play is over, nothing is left; the players pack up and go. The same is true once children stop playing a particular game.

From a psychological point of view, paracosms are interesting both because they are specialized examples of the childish – with its usually demeaning implications – imagination at work and because some of them leave permanent records. We know a good deal about Angria and Gondal and the games they allowed the Brontë children to play. The imaginary worlds that we describe in this book offer something like a freeze-frame of the imagination of children. Making up worlds is only one kind of imaginary activity – and a rare and specialized one at that – but it allows us to get a fix on what children do make up and invent as though it were in cold storage.

The origins of this book are due to Robert Silvey, who died in 1981. Silvey was a pioneer of audience research in this country; from 1932 to 1968 he was head of the BBC's Audience Research. It is fair to see him as one of the men who gave us the rules for the ratings battles of the television networks. As a child, Silvey created a world all of his own, the New Hentian States. He filled two notebooks with details of their mineral wealth, their legal system, their government, and their geography. On small index cards, he wrote out in neat handwriting front pages of the Hentian newspaper, which recorded such headline stories as 'Hentian Government in Crisis' and 'Flood Strikes Capital'. Silvey also drew some delicate maps of his self-made land. The 'Hentian States' is an example of Robert Silvey's fantasy childhood world which was a hobby verging on an obsession.

After he retired from the BBC, Silvey (1977) wrote an article in which he described what the Hentian States meant to him. He appealed for others who had had childhood worlds to get in contact with him, a plea he repeated in the *Author*, the *Friend*, and the *Observer*. He received

New
Hentian
States

Govt. Handbook of the ~~Federal~~ Republic of the Union of the New Hentian States for the year of our Lord nineteen hundred and twenty - one .

The cover of the handbook of Robert Silvey's imaginary world

Map of Robert Silvey's New Hentian States

many replies and began to send out questionnaires to obtain more details about these worlds. In 1979 he teamed up with a retired psychiatrist, Dr Stephen MacKeith, and together they set about analysing the data they had collected. When they had received questionnaires from fifty-seven individuals (a total of sixty-four worlds) they reviewed their 'catch'.

As they looked at the replies they had received, Silvey and MacKeith suggested that 'paracosmic imaginings' had four key characteristics. First, children must be able to distinguish between what they have imagined and what is real. Second, interest in the fantasy world must last for months or years; they weren't interested in passing worlds. Third, children had to be proud of the world and consistent about it. (Silvey and MacKeith were particularly determined that this kind of imaginative activity should not be confused with children having imaginary companions.) Lastly, children had to feel that the world mattered to them. These are, in fact, quite stringent criteria, ruling out those who merely 'toyed' with such worlds.

There are two ways of approaching the accounts of the imaginary worlds that we present. They can, and ought to, be read for pleasure and for their own sakes. Silvey and MacKeith collected an extraordinary mixture of fantasies from Teddyland, to elaborate railway systems, to African republics, to a couple of horsey girls who created a fantasy world based on a riding stable. Most of the people who replied to the advertisements had been born before 1950; it is telling that only two of them put their imaginary worlds in outer space. These worlds are worth discovering for their own odd logic, their charm and, sometimes, because one can glimpse through their structure the reasons the children needed them. We try to avoid over-simple analysis in this book of the sort that suggests that because children had an unhappy childhood, they devised a cuddlesome imaginary world where they were loved and in total control. But sometimes it seems clear that there were emotional factors at work which might push a creative child to make up this kind of world.

Silvey and MacKeith hoped, too, that the evidence they gathered would shed light on a subject little is known about – the development of the imagination. As we have tried to suggest, our attitudes to the imagination are ambivalent. Fantasies can make you a world famous author or a poor, unrespected 'schizo'.

Developmental psychology now sees play as a major topic. Moyles (1989) in the latest account of play cites about fifteen recent books on the subject. But this is a recent trend.

There is no psychologist we know of who is hostile to play. Play is a

Good Thing. Children ought to muck around with sand, pretend to be pirates, fire their fingers at each other, and love stories which transport them to another world. But despite play getting such a good press, most major theories of psychological development treat it as a peripheral subject. Consider Freud and Piaget, who have contributed the two most influential theories of child development. Piaget plotted the stages by which the child's intelligence develops. He believed that children advanced out of childish, egocentric thinking to an appreciation of logic. In the first two stages of development, *the sensory motor* and the *pre-operational period* (which last roughly till the child is 7), the child plays a great deal. But this should not fool the wise psychologist into thinking he has any imagination at all. Piaget argued formally that young children lack such a skill, though he did happen to believe that young children existed in a world of their own. For him, the phrase had its usual critical flavour: the adult world was real and ultimate. Piaget found that children up to the age of 7 were egocentric. They could see things only from their own immediate perspective. They could not conceive of how a scene looked from a different angle. In one of a series of famous experiments, Piaget showed children photographs of a mountain taken from down in the valley. Then he asked them to describe what the view would look like if they were standing on top. Children aged 4 tended to say it would look much the same; the shift of perspective was beyond them. Piaget equally suggested that though children pretend to be playing at soldiers this does not mean that they have sophisticated skills. Children under 7 are stuck by the situation in which they find themselves.

Piaget published his work originally in the 1920s and 1930s but it took until the 1970s for any fundamental criticisms to emerge. A series of experiments now suggest both that children under 7 are less handicapped and that they may be more imaginative. But Piaget's theory remains the dominant theory of intellectual development: the child moves through well-oiled stages to being a logical human who can perform quadratic equations and scientific experiments according to the laws of logic. Curiously, one of Piaget's children did develop a fantasy world; in one observation Piaget (1952) noted how surprised he was that researching this eighteenth-century land so fascinated T. For Piaget, it showed not the imagination at work but how children, as they got older, tried to be realistic in their play, to be as close to adults as possible.

15

If Piaget made little of childhood play, he was in good company. Freud wrote very little on play, assuming that children did play in order to develop motor and perceptual skills, and sometimes to express problems. But it didn't interest him much. Freud's book on jokes, the closest he comes to discussing the subject, is very much a book about adult jokes. Later on after the initial decades of psychoanalysis, child analysts did begin to be interested in play, especially D.W. Winnicott (1964), but Freud's theory of psychosexual development said little about it.

And where Piaget was interested in intellectual development, Freud was interested in psychosexual development. Play was interesting not in itself but for what it might reveal of the child's sexual development. One eminent psychoanalyst spent an afternoon with me in which he derided some American research into what kinds of sweets American children preferred. The American psychologists had not asked how the children played with the chocolate in their mouths. Did they bite it or suck it or play with it as long as they could? For the psychoanalyst that showed how superficial they were; for me it showed how one-track-minded he was. In one version, Freud saw the imagination as a kind of safety valve: the perfectly happy child would not need fantasies. In a second version Freud suggested that the child played in order to master a situation. Play was not central to his theory at all.

There has been a more positive attitude to play, fantasy, and the imagination since the 1970s. American psychologists see these as rich skills and argue this case, though the accent is still very much on the uses of play. For example Jerome Bruner (1977), a famous Harvard psychologist, has argued that children learn many crucial social skills through playing. But Bruner cannot help, it seems, focusing on what the child learns through play. It may be how to speak, a particular skill, or a set of social rules. In a now famous analysis of peekaboo, Bruner showed that in learning to play this game which mothers and children think fun, infants are being initiated into social life. Through peekaboo, they begin to grapple with give and take, with taking turns.

Bruner is certainly paradoxical. He accepts that children need to play. Through games, like peekaboo, the infant first learns to take the lead either by hiding behind a pillow or a blanket or handing it to the mother or father. For a 9-month-old baby it's no mean feat. But the paradox is interesting: there are two points to note. Bruner cannot quite free himself from the prejudices of Piaget and Freud, for whom play is not interesting in itself as a pointer to the imagination but only for what it tells us about either logical or emotional development. Later analysts like D.W. Winnicott were more willing to see fun in play but Winnicott remains an exception. The second paradox we have mentioned before. Nothing remains of children's play: it fleets by. Bruner does not seem to value much of what children produce in play. It is the act of playing that is important. Never mind the quality, just get on with any game.

In the light of such views, it's not surprising that psychologists are far from offering any theory of the imagination; what work there has been suggests that what children can create is firmly linked to their intellectual development. Researchers have suggested stages in the development of play that are connected with intellectual development (Garvey 1982). Using naturalistic observation and experiments, it's been possible to see the kinds of conditions that both help and inhibit imaginative play. Most children will take time to play well with a strange child. As a consequence, children can be divided into those who are good fantasizers and those who are poor fantasizers. There seem to be clear advantages to being a good fantasizer.

Singer and Singer (1977) looked at children who were good at producing fantasies. They have better concentration, are less aggressive, and take more pleasure in what they do than children who fantasize less. Tower and Singer (1980) argued that children who were adept at imagining would develop better social and cognitive skills. They would integrate experiences better, learn the differences between what were inner and outer experiences, learn to organize information, become more reflective and, finally, high fantasizers would have superior concentration. The social benefits would also be lavish because they would become more sensitive to others. Tower and Singer (1980) recommended that parents learn to play fantasy games with their children so that the child 'is generating and executing ideas based on its own experience in a context of mutual respect, interest and absence of criticism'. They couldn't specify how to create this mood of fantasy. Freyberg (1981) offered various hints on how to develop creativity but he concentrated on how to do it with materials.

In a practical review of how schools use play which makes many useful recommendations, Moyles (1989) praises the use of the imagination and quotes Claxton (1984) that to be creative you have to dare to be different. Moyles adds, 'Being creative requires time and imagination both of which most children have available to them. More importantly being creative requires self trust, some knowledge receptivity, a sense of nonsense, and the ability to play' (1989: 80). This is a long list but Moyles is sure that they are all 'well within the realms of childhood and many of which need to be engendered with greater vigour in the context of school and education' (1989: 80).

It is hard to escape the conclusion that Moyles remains rather vague both in her praise of play and her notions of how to promote it. The problem is familiar. It is hard to specify the specific gain in skills. It is hard to work out just how to coax children into being more imaginative. As a result, it is important to examine in some detail the products of children's imagination that we do have – and to value them. All too often, developmental psychologists write as if the only purpose of any kind of play is to enable the child to master 'real', serious skills.

This is not the place to review theories of play but it is worth recording one exception to the rule that the products of children's play aren't valued: children's drawings. Like imaginary worlds, children's drawings survive to be studied. Initially psychologists who studied such drawings were interested in what they revealed of the state of mind of the child: they were not regarded as art. In many ways, the study of children's drawings owed a lot to the development of a test for adults called the Rorschach, which consists of a series of inkblots. Subjects have to say if the inkblot on the page reminds them of a penis or a policeman or a dowager duchess in an Ascot hat. Their answers betray their deep obsessions and can indicate whether they are mad, sane, depressed, or depraved. It then began to occur to analysts dealing with children that children's drawings were a kind of Rorschach. In what were later called their 'artful scribbles', children revealed what they were really thinking about. During the Troubles in Belfast, it was found that children drew more pictures with guns, tanks, and funerals in them, revealing that such violence was not only on their street but also on their mind. More interestingly, children who lived in safe areas untouched by the Troubles filled their drawings with even more violence than those who lived near the centre of the action. Fear produced these 'fantasies' (McWhirter 1987).

Children's drawings have continued to be studied. As Howard Gardner (1984) points out in his study of them, they have been seen in two ways. First, as information about the state of mind of the children; second, as a kind of art. As modern painters like Klee produced child-like art, it became possible to ask how 'childish' art ranked among the great canvases of the world. Psychologists like

Gardner certainly discovered some very talented young artists such as Nadia, who was autistic but, at 9, an immaculate draughtswoman. Her picture of a wiry horse stays in the mind. Gardner also reproduced pictures by 'normal' gifted children. His evaluation of the imaginative efforts of child artists is interesting because it *respects* their work. Most psychologists who have studied play have tended to see it only as a process of development. What children do, the artistic (or creative) products, in themselves, isn't serious. It is studied only because it reveals part of growing up.

The other recent interesting development has been Parsons' (1988) attempt to develop a theory of how children and young adults understand art. Parsons argues that such understanding develops in a series of stages. At first, children judge art very perceptually; they have favourite colours like yellow or red. Then they begin to grasp that paintings can represent things and people, but they tend to judge the representation in terms of a simple realism. This is very evident till they are about 9, after which they do begin to understand that a work of art reflects feelings and that an important part of understanding it is feeling the feelings it's meant to convey. Parsons (1988) considers the responses of teenagers, young adults, and even people in their 30s. He argues that not everyone gets beyond the stage of responding uncritically according to the feelings that paintings evoke.

It should be clear by now why the evidence gathered by Silvey and MacKeith is so interesting, such fun, and more than fun. They have put together records of some sixty-four paracosms. In most of the instances, people replied to letters and questions put by Silvey so that the descriptions that follow are, in fact, memories. In a few cases, however, the raw data remain – exercise books filled with obsessive details by a 12-year-old who is dreaming up a constitution for his country or a timetable for the universal railway, maps which are clearly labours of love. And they prompt many questions. What makes a child devote so much time to making up a world? Is it to get away from adults? How convincing is the world? What happens with it? Adults are only too ready to presume that children will use it to create fantasies of control. Think of *Billy Liar*, which is admittedly an adult fictional imaginary world (Waterhouse and Hall 1960). Billy, who cannot muster the courage to leave the North of England, dreams of the perfect Republic where he is a glorious master decked in a glorious uniform. In his head, he is in control. One of the interesting things to emerge from all these stories is that children have many *different* motives for setting up their dream worlds.

The Temple of Jupiter from the Model in the Cathedral Museum.

This drawing and the one opposite are from the forty-page illustrated booklet describing an entirely imaginary Cathedral.

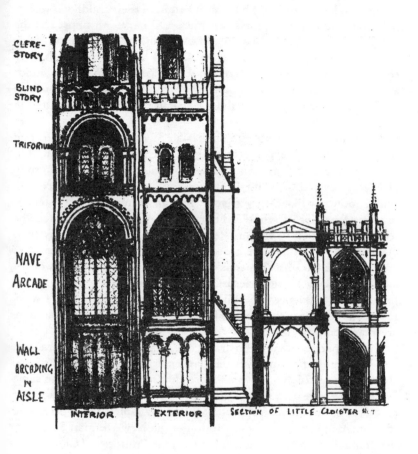

CLERE-
STORY

BLIND
STORY

TRIFORIUM

NAVE
ARCADE

WALL
ARCADING
IN
AISLE

INTERIOR   EXTERIOR   SECTION OF LITTLE CLOISTER & T

'The Nave of Pinchester Cathedral is one of the finest examples of Norman Architecture in the Country. Built between 1100 and 1150, it is remarkable for its height and grandeur. Especially noteworthy is the great height of the Nave Arcade, (nearly 60ft), and the spacious Triforium, which is vaulted similarly to the Aisles.

'The lovely series of Decorated windows in the Aisles were inserted about 1330, and the magnificent Nave vault about 1380.'

21

In many ways, the material we publish is unique. Famous writers, having achieved fame, become candidates for the Ph.D. industry. The Brontës' worlds have been described, discussed, and dissected; every comma they ever scribbled has value. Men like Peter Ustinov, W.H. Auden, and Jacques Borel have seen details of their childhood worlds published. Our contributors are more ordinary; we approach the question differently. The majority of contributions remain anonymous and, in only two cases, could it be claimed that these 'imaginative' children became famous. As a result, these records of imaginary worlds are a rich source for understanding how children's imaginations can work and can develop among those who don't go on to make glittering creative careers.

In an attempt to classify the material, Silvey and MacKeith tried to group it both according to ages and according to themes. It is certainly true that some basic themes do recur. First, there is a group of worlds centred on animals and on toys. A second group centres round countries like Silvey's New Hentian States. A third category involves fantasies of schools. Fourth, and it is odd how dated the technology is, some worlds are 'technological', mainly railway systems of various sorts. Fifth, there are some worlds grouped round a theatre, and finally, a few miscellaneous ones. The very fact that the 'worlds' fall easily into such categories is interesting because it seems to reflect the different influences on children. Their imagination didn't work in a vacuum. One of the curious facts about this collection is that there are many cute worlds but no truly zany ones.

Each separate chapter illustrates one particular kind of paracosm and each subsection outlines the particular imaginary world of one child. Very occasionally two or more children have shared the same fantasy. We have used a lot of direct quotations both from the answers to Silvey's questionnaire, and, where available, from preserved 'documents', such as the constitution of the New Hentian States, or the dramatic exchange of letters between the President of Chimbongo and his aides concerning the appalling behaviour of the previous regime. This emphasis is quite deliberate. Psychologists tend to rush into deep analysis before collecting very much raw material. Here the products of these children's imaginations are complicated, odd, and interesting in themselves. They suggest a link between the age of the creator of a world and its complexity but there isn't enough evidence to erect a complete theory of the stages of the imagination. Nevertheless, we do draw some conclusions in the last chapter about what these worlds might mean and MacKeith has outlined in the Appendices a description of some stages in imaginative development.

Finally, a word of advice. Adults – keep out. One of the recurrent themes to emerge is that children wanted to keep the worlds they created to themselves. The child wanted to be 'in a world of his own' and had gone to the effort of constructing it. Many readers of this book are likely to be parents; they may well feel inspired to rush to their children and see if they can teach them this exciting new game. Piaget used to complain that Americans studied psychology only in order to see what they could get children to do younger and better. Adults ought to leave children to get on with their imaginary worlds by themselves. Only if we respect their privacy will they be able at leisure to toy with their constitutions and legal systems, appoint themselves ministers, and design locomotives and space stations. If children still have imaginary worlds – and it's hard to believe that they don't – some of those creating their most secret places must be setting them now in outer space beyond AD 2001.

Many of those who answered Silvey and MacKeith's notices and enquiries seemed relieved that someone was interested. It is easy for us to fancy that only weird children can have an imaginary world. As far as one can make out from the fifty-seven replies, the majority of those who got in touch were normal and relatively successful. Silvey's files are full of letters typed on United Nations paper or on that of various ministries. Nevertheless, one has the feeling that for most of them conjuring up such a world seemed slightly odd and obsessive. If anyone found out who wasn't too sympathetic, they might laugh. As the whole subject is fraught with these slightly delicate tensions, adults shouldn't muscle in.

If your child has a secret world, do you want to know? Do you have a right to know? Perhaps not.

At the end of reading this book, we don't believe that anyone will know just how the imagination develops or what it is that makes quite small children (younger than 6 and upwards) able to fabricate worlds. But the reader will have enjoyed a wealth of childhood fantasies and have some sense of the fact that if we are ever to understand how the imagination develops, we shall have to be able to understand how young children find the skill and motivation to conjure up such remarkable places.

Chapter One

TOYS

Toys are meant to be a prod to the imagination. All too often, children seem to use toys literally. Some psychologists even suggest that play 'progresses' as it becomes more 'real'. Tiny children don't know how to use a toy horse at all; a little later, infants know what makes a toy horse and use it correctly; with a little cognitive maturity, toddlers know they can pretend anything is a horse – a rag, a lump of plastic, a parent. But, then, reality starts its demands. The toy must look more and more like a horse to deserve being played with as a horse. We grow up literal. In searching for ways of grouping these paracosms, it soon became clear that many of them had their origins in objects or toys. They were the scaffolding, and spark, for a new world. And, as we shall see, many of the children slowly came to see that was a handicap.

KATE – TEDDY RULES

When Kate was about 7, her brother Brian, who was 10, recruited her into an imaginary world which was to absorb them both for the next three years. Brian was the initiator throughout, and although Kate joined in with enthusiasm *she* lost interest when Brian outgrew their private world.

Petsland consisted of three cities: Petsville for the larger toys, Juville for those of medium size, and Hamville for the tiny ones. Its first President, a large teddy bear called Edward Smythe-Holand, took to drink and eventually fetched up in jail. His successor was a pig-shaped rubber hot-water bottle known as Percy. Petsland had a written constitution. Although it did not last long enough to outgrow its roots in toys, it was important to the children that the events which took place there were plausible. Often, they were like happenings in the 'real' world. For example one teddy bear proved to be a gifted entrepreneur, setting up a number of flourishing enterprises. Eventually he created a merchant bank. He became Financial Adviser to the President.

Crime was rare, and usually due to high spirits. The inhabitants of Petsland were extremely hard-working; it was an offence for anyone *not* to have employment unless they were at home looking after children. The children were all educated in a perfect example of a comprehensive school over which a Miss Peabody presided. Kate appeared to identify with her.

Kate does not think her brother was inspired by any outside source in creating this private world. They both regarded it as a shared secret: no other children were told about it. Their parents knew; their father, in particular, was encouraging because 'he thought this form of play preferable to watching electric trains going round and round'. Petsland and its activities provided an inexhaustible source of interest for the children. It lifted the restrictions of the 'real' world. 'We were "in charge" of Petsland and could manipulate its destiny.' They had to care for twenty or thirty 'real entities (real to us, that is), that we could devote ourselves to'.

In her replies, Kate was not very detailed. She described herself as a tomboy and her brother as 'very virginal'. Her home and its values were conventionally lower-middle class; they were *Daily Telegraph* readers. There were 'plenty of books around' and music was important in the family. Their parents believed in education and that was one reason her father supported it. Kate doesn't think it affected her development in any very definite way – a childhood fantasy that ended in childhood.

HOLLY – CAT KINGDOM

The fantasy experience of Holly falls into two distinct phases: the first before, and the second after, her family moved from the suburbs to the country. She was about 6. For several years before this, her private world was a country called Branmail to which

> access could only be obtained by scaling a height called Bumpety Banks. Apart from myself, all the inhabitants were cats. Within this nation was one family who were my especial friends, consisting of father, elder daughter, Kitty, and younger offspring. Kitty

was a sort of anti-heroine . . . the perpetrator of any offence I had myself committed!

Holly's fantasy was a solitary preoccupation. Her parents were aware of it and they encouraged her. She would act out stories about it, but was never conscious, either then or in the second phase, of any constraints upon her imagination which might have been imposed by a need to look plausible.

Branmail 'somehow faded out' when she was about 6; thereafter she 'created many worlds which again were consistently important' to her till, at the age of 13,

> I decided in the space of one afternoon that I could not go on living in a childish world of non-existent people. This was a distressing decision and I found that I continued to talk to figments of my imagination at times when I was not concentrating on anything else . . . to some extent I still do so.

The succeeding private worlds were primarily personal. Holly would invent stories, which she later came 'to write in my head', setting them in different imaginary landscapes. These tended to be bleak. Holly herself was always one of the characters; others had qualities, like being a super athlete, which she would very much have liked to possess or would do things, like horse riding or mountain climbing, which were not available to her.

These worlds were creations of solitude, though she did once allow her younger sister to participate in one of them. At about 10, they became completely secret. In these years, Holly says, she 'did not relate too well to her immediate family'. Looking back, she thinks that her worlds enabled her to 'avoid noticing' her problems, and to 'withdraw from the real world where I felt I could not influence events'. But at the time 'I was just doing it because I enjoyed it'.

In the first suburban phase, Holly sees herself as having been a bright, curious, energetic, and light-hearted little girl, imaginative, out-going, self-confident, and single-minded. The qualities which she thinks characterized her later were paradoxical. She was physically adventurous but timid in personal relationships. With shyness came self-doubts. She was at her happiest when she was alone with her beloved dog. She describes this as a time when happiness and unhappiness were intermingled. When she was younger she was happy without qualifications.

Holly's family was inward-looking. She had two sisters, one very much younger than herself. Both her parents and the great-aunt, who came to live with them when they moved into the country, were university-educated, but 'outside their specialities their horizons were not particularly wide'. Their values and attitudes were those of an impoverished but consciously 'middle-class' family. They were Church of England but attitudes towards the Church were fairly balanced.

Holly was seldom reasoned with, she was usually 'just told' how she should behave. When she was little, she could discuss anything with her parents, but later this became impossible. It troubled her to hear her parents make derogatory remarks about close relatives. She 'did not really like school. . . . For various reasons I felt "different" from other children' and with few exceptions she did not get on very well with children of her own age.

Holly provides an instructive contrast between Branmail, her private world during the 3–6 age period, and her series of fantasies or paracosms between 6 and 13. The young world was full of cats, and was characterized by a good deal of 'acting out'. When she got older, she used stories to fulfil wishes or compensate for feelings of inadequacy, so it's not surprising that Holly was distressed when she gave up these stories at the age of 13. It did leave a mark. Even as an adult, Holly sometimes talked to imaginary people, though she didn't say if that was mainly at times of stress.

LAURA – DREAMS

Laura was between 6 and 8 years old when either she, or one of her two sisters (twins, two years older), had a dream which became the basis for a joint private world. Each of them contributed to its development with 'dreams' of their own and it lasted, Laura thinks, for about a year. The characters formed a kind of community. The dream world Laura describes is not unusual but what is extraordinary is the development over a year of shared dreams between three children. To some extent, since their father wrote down the dreams, the children may have dreamed to order. Her 'rough synopsis' of the 'dream', as recollected fifty years later, reads:

> They were about two grown-ups called Witchie and Edgar who looked after a hundred children. They and the children were constantly on the move trying to find a big enough home. Edgar was

a motherly person who wore her hair in plaited earphones, and Witchie was a friendly witch who was always helpful as she could take off on her broomstick to explore. On one occasion she took Yellow Stephen (a live version of our teddy bear) with her and went to the moon, but found it too cold and with no fruit or vegetables, so it was proclaimed unsuitable.

As well as the teddy bear there were characters based on books. Laura's father used to read to them *The Midnight Folk* by John Masefield, which influenced the witch in their dreams. So did another of Masefield's characters, Edgar.

When Laura read the account of the dream she had provided to Silvey, she felt disappointed because 'it seems to me now rather prosaic and almost plausible. My *feeling* about the dreams is that they were filled with curious and exciting imagery. The episode of the ''Trizzer Knee'' for instance seems very pale and dull when written down.' Here is the disappointingly pale Trizzer Knee:

> They lived for a while in a very large mushroom with rooms and staircases, but found it damp and depressing. Once more on their travels, they found the 'Trizzer Knee'. This was like a gigantic trouser-leg with an elevator in it which travelled up and down, stopping at different levels. On one level was the giant, Ogo-Pogo, who had only one eye and kept a sweet-shop, and on another level hot soup was dished out for all the 100 children.
>
> Finally they settled down in a very large house; but the 'dreams' continue with more adventures. Edgar had difficulty in keeping her eye on everyone and with the housework, so she enlisted the help of a beetle-like animal called Doctor Dee, who moved smoothly about under the table at and after meals, eating up the crumbs.

The 'dreams' were a bond between the three sisters; but they were, in any case, a close and affectionate group, particularly the twins, much given to giggling.

Their father, a professor of theology, wrote down the 'dreams' and this 'made us feel rather important'. One of the sisters who was good at drawing provided illustrations. Their mother also wrote books; it was a serious household. Comics were frowned upon though sometimes they bought them with pocket money. Laura doesn't think, once the dream sharing was over, that it affected them.

MATILDA – MATRIARCHS AND CLOWNS

When Matilda was 8 or 9, she and a sister, four years younger, began a continuous bedtime story which went on for two or three years. It was about

> a community, a family, with myself, a matriarch, at the head. It was called Mrs-es and was largely a fantasy of adulthood. The major figures in our world were the matriarchs; we had husbands, who were puppet figures, and my sister (who in the game was a neighbour) had a renegade son . . . but on the whole it was we who were important.

Clown hot-water bottles, given them for Christmas, served as husbands.

'The home was a cave, fitted with all mod cons, somewhere in Scotland.' Later, the cave was abandoned for a houseboat. Mrs-es was contemporary; the children had no interest in its geography or history.

> Playing Mrs-es consisted of improvised dialogues on a theme decided at the start of bedtime, interspersed with new things appearing in the dialogue. This having been done, the dialogue could continue. For instance, if we went to a ball, there would be time set aside to describe what we were wearing, what the ballroom, and the banquet which followed the ball, were like, etc. . . . The dialogue included the bed toys which were our children, and the clowns, who were our husbands. . . . It was a world remote from the events of the day.

Matilda has no recollection of feeling the free play of her imagination constrained by the need to be plausible. 'The life arose from the creation of characters', not the other way round. 'I found it fun, and relaxing, just to let my mind wander round our world. . . . It was not a secret. . . . When my parents would call up the stairs for us to stop talking, we would call back that we were only playing Mrs-es.'

For Matilda, the act of creating Mrs-es was more important than what she created.

> I certainly put myself in an imaginary position of control in this game; it is certain that I was a nervous child, fearful of failure and of falling short. Maybe I made a world in which I knew I would be right, without my parents. . . . I suspect I was opting out of the

strains imposed by new babies, maternal ill-health, parental financial anxieties, and, generally, the eldest child syndrome.

She had vivid memories of 'standing outside of' herself as a child, of seeing herself 'from the outside'. She was a musical child, considered gifted, and something of a 'loner'. While she enjoyed her school days, she very often felt herself excluded; but this was mutual, as she often felt her school-mates 'were stupid'.

During the war, when her father was serving overseas, the family lived with Matilda's maternal grandparents, to whom she felt very close. When her father came home, she drew closer to him (he was a teacher) than to her mother, who had had little education and was fearful of 'going outside her own sphere'.

It was a moral family. 'Telling lies was a great sin. Having five children . . . was rather disgusting . . . I could not see why.' They were a church-going family but not 'pi'; they said prayers at bedtime. 'I don't remember, but I expect I was "just told" how to behave.' She and her mother were not intimate; but in her teens her father found it stimulating to talk to her 'about the kind of issues my mother could not, or would not, discuss with him'.

In retrospect, Matilda sees her childhood as containing patches of both happiness and unhappiness; but at the time, she says, 'I made no such distinctions. I just "was".' Again, as she grew up, she could detect few lingering influences of the fantasy.

PHILIP - A DEVIL OF A PLACE

In the few years before going away to prep school, Philip shared a private world with his brother, who was his junior by two years. 'It was a mythical, but contemporary country, usually an island; a floating island which could be moved about. Its shape changed every time we drew it or talked about it.' This island, Animal-land, 'was inhabited by Golliwogs, Humpty-dumpties, animals, dolls (which we hated), babies (which we disliked), and Masters (we were Master I and Master II)'. The boys made the Golliwogs from coloured wools. 'One size, about 6 inches high, we classified as devils with names like Methistopheles (*sic*), Satan, Beel-ze-bub etc. There were forty-seven Golliwogs in the end, and twelve Humpties – all named.'

'Animal-land' was largely a continuous bedtime story, for the boys did not act out its events. They would tell one another episodes, usually with much laughter and noise until a grown-up told us to shut up after lights out. We then continued in whispers. Anyone we liked or admired from time to time got included in the stories we made up, but we never told them. People we disliked were sometimes brought in, but they usually got on badly!

Family experiences, but not events in the wider world, were incorporated in the stories.

Philip thinks their private world was a spontaneous creation, not, as far as he knows, imitated by any of their friends. It was not secret; they took no trouble to conceal it. He has no recollection of any conflict between his imagination and needing to be plausible. He certainly derived a great deal of fun from their private world, without ever having become deeply involved emotionally. He doubts if it played a particularly important role in his development.

Philip recalls he was an energetic little boy, good at games, conscientious, reliable but solitary. His prep school headmaster described him as the perfect introvert, 'the closest oyster I have ever encountered in forty years teaching'. Philip particularly liked stories about animals, myths, and legends, and natural scenery 'which gave me a yearning for I know not what – God perhaps'. He doesn't remember hating anything except 'injustice, cruelty and the deliberate infliction of pain'.

The boys loved their mother but were slightly in awe of her. She was widowed in the First World War, but hardly poor for there was always a staff of several servants, including a nurse for the two children. Philip did not say what the nurse made of the bedtime stories or if they were made up, because the children were left to their own devices. Philip describes his childhood as 'happy, but I would not wish to go back to it'.

CAROLE – FRISKYLAND

Friskyland, the fantasy which Carole shared with her brother, came into being when she was 8 years old and her brother 10. It 'was a pleasant land, somehow not far away, but out of sight until you were there, and then you were amongst its green and pleasant fields and undulating hills . . . there were no houses in Friskyland, but very many Friskies'.

These 'were all children . . . perhaps three inches tall'. They were not bothered by clothes but weren't quite naked either, as they all wore a kind of white singlet with no sleeves so that their arms and the greater part of their legs were bare. Carole and her brother were themselves Friskies while they were in Friskyland, but 'did not talk to the [imaginary] Friskies or play with them but accepted them as an essential part of the place'.

Among the other inhabitants were Big Dears and Little Dears, 'who always performed kind actions and did nice things'. Unlike Friskies, Dears had toy counterparts; 'we made [them] out of cotton-wool which we coloured'. Big Dears were perhaps ten times as tall as Friskies, but Little Dears, who never grew into Big Dears, were far smaller. Dears were not of human shape as they looked like 'elongated spheres' and had four feet. They were covered with fur, looked not unlike hedgehogs but their fur was the colour of a rainbow. Nevertheless, they had human personalities.

Adventures often consisted of escaping from Naughts; these 'were much the same size and shape as Dears' and similarly constructed, but they were all painted black. 'Naughts were horrible creatures, much to be feared, so we ran from them . . . though I'm not quite sure what they might have done'. There were, in addition, Stones,

> as much alive as Friskies, Dears and Naughts. . . . There were windows and doors in their smooth grey sides. . . . You could go through a door and get inside a Stone to be safe, so we did this when Naughts appeared. . . . From inside we looked out of a window on our frustrated enemy. . . . Inside the Stones land, too, was a wonderfully equipped gymnasium, just like the one in our father's Technical College, where we would hang on ropes. We sometimes got inside a Stone just for that purpose.
>
> By mutual consent my brother and I often went to Friskyland, describing our activities to each other, though we may not have had identical pictures of it in our minds' eye. It was a place where we wanted to go though I have little memory of what we did there; but I can remember constructing a huge bonfire, with a long passage right into the middle for the purpose of lighting it – but I do not think it was ever lit.

It was larger than any real bonfire.

Carole believed Friskyland was a spontaneous invention though, years later, she could pin its origins down to seeing a picture of Tom in *The Water-Babies* in a white singlet. Certainly her parents didn't make up the land for them and didn't encourage it, but it wasn't a secret.

The last activity in Friskyland was never finished . . . it has remained in my mind ever since as a vague eventuality still to be completed. . . . It was the erection of a complicated system of overhead walkways, supported by pylons, and so designed that only Friskies could use them. Perhaps Friskyland was becoming too complicated . . . for without plan or comment we just stopped talking about it.

Carole thinks this must have happened when she was about 10.

Although Friskyland was fantastic and the children's imagination had free rein, they 'did not go against natural laws. . . . Water did not run uphill and we could not fly, etc.' It was private, but not secret; their parents knew about it, but didn't interfere in any way. It had been a spontaneous creation. No other children had a hand in it; nor, as far as Carole can remember, did any other children imitate it. She does not see their paracosm as having been a compensation for unsatisfactory personal relationships; their home was a harmonious one and she was never irked by what she felt to be unnecessary restrictions. But she does see it as an escape from the rather dreary surroundings in which they lived in a northern industrial town. The children revelled in their annual holiday in the country. In retrospect, Carole thinks the satisfaction they derived from Friskyland was 'doing things rather better than in real life, and . . . having assured safety inside a Stone, with Big Dears and Little Dears to take care of you'.

Carole's father was the principal of a technical college and her mother was an ex-teacher with 'progressive ideas'. 'My brother and I were good friends – mother would see to that; but we were very different and I rather think the interest he took in Friskyland might have been to please a younger sister.' As young children they were much together but drifted apart by the time Carole was 10 years old. He preferred reading mathematics and philosophy; she preferred playing in the garden.

Their house was full of books, Shakespeare, Dickens, the Waverley novels, encyclopaedias for all interests and Carole read everything from *Lavengro* to *The Boys' Own Paper*. Her parents were also musical. They were 'believers', but not punctilious church-goers; 'they never spoke of religious matters'. Friskyland did not feel to Carole to be a land that the children invented to get away from the adults. Adventures were sometimes deliciously frightening, though Carole could not remember any, but there was no danger of the children starting to think Friskyland was anything but a fantasy. Carole doesn't think it influenced her life.

ALICE – PAPERING A WORLD

When Alice was about 10, she and her brother, three years younger, began to create an imaginary world. To begin with, the 'paracosm' was based on toys, mostly paper dolls; but 'once we realised we could draw and write about the characters, we were emancipated from the toys'. Drawing was important in their play. For a time the children were content with inventing what they called 'communes' – relatively short-lived groups of characters who interacted. They were inspired by the comedies they heard on the radio, by the novels of P.G. Wodehouse and Angela Thirkell, and even by cartoons in the *News Chronicle*. It was a rigid society with proper ladies and improper drudges who had to slave, fetch and carry. There were chickens too and, once the Dionne quins were born, they were slotted in and lived in a 'candy shell bed'. The story of the commune evolved into a more domestic saga whose characters enjoyed more staying power. Its setting owed much to the northern industrial area in which they lived. Their imaginary principal family, 'lower-middle/upper-working-class', was similar to the children's own. Its central character was a youngish woman called Penelope: 'blonde, blue eyed, beautiful, bossy, very competent and very domestic'. At first her role varied; she could be at one time a film-star, at another a part-time worker in an office, and at another 'just a housewife'. The children were no more bothered by these metamorphoses than they were by Penelope's frequent marriages, sometimes in veils, sometimes in Persian lamb coats. Later, Alice 'tried to rationalize things and expunge the film-star', changes which her younger brother was not ready for.

Penelope belonged to a 'ramifying family . . . some were poor, but all genteel . . . one branch had married into the squirearchy'. She had two daughters and a husband (Hector) who was very much 'a man of affairs though his profession was never certain. At one time he was a publisher. One of the daughters, Daphne, was the archetypal naughty little sister.' The saga included evacuees (it was then early in the Second World War). There was a feckless Irish family, the McMeegans, who drank and had frequent flamboyant, and rather fascinating weddings.

(There was an unpopular community of immigrant Irish Catholic workers near the children's home.) There was a Lady Bountiful with a 'Paxton-type garden' and a habit of stealing people's doors. There was a male character, Bones, whose distinction was that he sang soprano and occasionally produced *La Forza del destino*; Emmanuel Poker, the archetypal fixer; and an Italian restaurateur. Men were in short supply (another reflection of wartime life); the absent men 'were always said to be ill and away living in a place called Fleurette Isle'.

Much of the activity was romantic. Unlike Friskyland, Alice's characters were always falling in and out of love. Maids had a particular fancy for French soldiers, but there were few battles. As Alice developed her imaginary world during the war, 'we yearned for peace, plenty, brothers who did not drudge and people who never died'. In writing to reply to Robert Silvey's questionnaire, Alice said that till her brother married at the age of 31 they occasionally wrote about the activities of their characters. She pointed out, too, that when they stopped relying on the dolls as an impetus to the imagination that 'we were emancipated from the toys'. Then they could become truly mythical.

This private world was not secret. The children's parents knew about it but did not interfere, though they actively encouraged the children's drawing, which became a central feature. Alice was sure that their world did encourage them 'to ferret out information, and puzzle out problems' for themselves, and that it did help them cope better with problems.

Alice was reading at 5, and was 'passionately fond of myths and legends'. The home was 'full of books, mostly Mother's', and the children were encouraged to take an interest in the arts. Discipline, in theory at least, was based on 'reasoning'. Discussions between parents and children were free-ranging, 'even about sex, though this was difficult'. Alice's school-days were happy, although she so hated organized games.

Do imaginary worlds run in families? Alice records a recent contact with two nephews, aged 11 and 8. 'They had large quantities of Toyland currency, coins and notes; and maps and coats of arms of several countries, all with very small populations.' Alice believed that this meant they had imbibed the 'small is beautiful' philosophy. Three years ago, having watched the television documentary series on the history of the Women's Rights Movement, *Shoulder to Shoulder*, one child invented a sort of feminist *corps d'élite* which he called the

Doris Minervas, who, he said, carried tommy-guns though they 'only pursued men who were unkind to their wives'.

We thought we would end some chapters with an account by a child of an ongoing fantasy world, for the adults we've just recorded might be embellishing the mists of their memory – or making it up nostalgically.

SIMONE

Simone is a very intelligent and articulate child of 9. She told us she had an imaginary world and that she would answer questions about it.

She said she 'was just 8' when it all began and that she 'kept it a secret for about a year'. She told her teacher and two of her friends but 'didn't want anyone else to know'. Asked to describe her imaginary world, she said:

> I never really imagined what it was. It has lots of suburban houses, coloured yellow, pink and blue. They are all in rows like streets. They all have toys' names on them for addresses. There are lots of other buildings. One of them is where the toys get their passports to go to other countries. There are lots of shops. The toys all have to be a week old or over to live in Toytown. The birds are all striped different colours. There are lots of big green trees, but the only flowers are rhododendrons. They have them in all different colours everywhere. All the toys drink only lemonade and they all eat peanuts only. Each house has a kitchen, two bedrooms (one for them and one for another toy if they come to stay), one living room and one dining room. They don't have any garden, but there is a park at the end of each street. There's no public transportation but they each design their own cars. We don't keep track of dates, but I'd say it was in the present. It's not like other places I've been to. The sun always shines. It never rains, but the rhododendrons survive. There's a special language. Each toy has his own individual language, but when he speaks to another toy they can understand each other.
>
> It's all like everyday life, but it's strange too because it's not like *our* everyday life. I drew one picture of it. I make up something tragic or something wonderful happening once in a while. I use it just to dream in.

Of its origin, Simone said:

For my eighth birthday someone gave me a toy. There was a picture with it. That gave me the idea of where it could live. I just thought, I'll make it live in such and such a place and I thought of all my other toys and where they might live. Slowly I just made up a whole town.

Had she any idea of what made it fun? 'It helps my imagination and it gives me new ideas to play with my toys. It gives me something to think and dream about when I'm bored.'

Simone is an only child and of herself she said:

I like to be around people. Sometimes I can't stand to be alone. I like noise, people doing things, excitement. I'm very adventurous but shy when I first meet people. I like to read exciting stories and draw exciting pictures. I like badminton but not other games and I don't like P.E. I'm very good at making things as long as they aren't too difficult.

Most bits of my life are happy, but some bits are sad.

Chapter Two

PARTICULAR PLACES AND LOCAL COMMUNITIES

Some imaginary worlds are essentially 'local'. They are based on specific institutions such as a farm, a boarding school, an orphanage, a riding school, or a repertory theatre. In most of these the play of personal relationships tends to be important. These, too, are commonly shared with one or two siblings or friends. And as children grow older, their fantasies get more sophisticated and mirror an increasingly complex world.

JOY – CLOSE FAIRIES

Joy was the youngest of three sisters. They lived with their parents in the depths of the country, and when she was about 7 she began imagining that a specific part of a wood was Fairyland. 'I never saw the characters of my land because, being fairies, they were too shy to come out.' She thinks she took over the idea from her sister who was five years older, but 'I liked to go there on my own. I think we took a few people there . . . who we felt would respect our world.' Her sister took a girlfriend to the magic part of the wood. 'Sometimes we would walk there with adults.' Then not telling them would be part of her pleasure.

She imagined that the fairies lived in

mossy tree-stumps . . . I made, or helped to make, homes for them, tidying up the leaves and making doorways out of holes in the tree-stumps. The most important part of the world was that it already existed; all I had to do was to sustain my belief in it and keep it as entirely natural and secret as possible, so that the fairies wouldn't mind and might some day appear. There was a magic tree where you could climb up and wish. And you had to apologize if you stepped on a dead branch and broke it. You also had *not* to walk on the mossy bits if possible, because anything mossy belonged to the fairies.

Joy's imagination had been stimulated by Mrs Molesworth's *The Ruby Ring*, and by the illustrations she had seen in books of fairy stories and nursery rhymes. She was also much impressed by 'an old Colonel who lived in a café where my father used to stop sometimes. . . . This old man had taken pictures of fairies at the bottom of *his* garden and talked about them quite seriously.' Joy's fantasy faded away when she was about 10.

Her fantasy reflected her passions. Nature and natural things were then, and always have been, the source of Joy's deepest pleasure: 'being in touch with the changing seasons . . . and being at times very moved by the actual physical presence of a landscape'. She thinks that as a child she derived aesthetic pleasure from shapes and colours and textures. 'It was an unconscious kind of communing with nature, I suppose, . . . a good feeling, a rightness about my feet on the ground among the leaves, and touching the tree-trunks, and looking at the water flowing in the stream'.

But Fairyland was also 'a place to escape to. A place away from the noisy public life of the family. It was always comforting. Nothing dangerous happened. It was a very gentle world.' She liked playing there alone as much as when her sister was with her. Her sister was a tomboy, whereas 'I was rather cowardly and afraid of heights. . . . Fairyland was sanctuary.' It gave her 'an aesthetic pleasure in shapes, colours and textures'. She felt right, being with nature, 'touching the tree-trunks and looking at the water flowing in the stream'.

Joy loved being read to by her mother and being carried by her father. She hated parties, riding in a gymkhana and, surprisingly, given her fairy escapades, being left away from home. Fairyland had to be very close. But she was aware of contradictions: at least, years later, when she wrote down her imaginary world.

On the one hand, Joy describes herself between 7 and 10, as 'timid', 'imaginative', 'solitary', and 'unmechanically minded'. But she had fantasies 'about screaming and shouting at my father. I was not good at letting out my anger . . . and would sulk instead. . . . I lacked confidence in a worldly sense.' She had fears that her parents would be killed in a car accident or that her father, parking her in the car

while he shopped, 'would go off and leave me'. But she 'didn't feel
all that much a need to "withdraw", as I lived a pretty quiet life in
the country, especially when my sisters were at school'. Joy looks back
on her childhood as a happy time.

Joy believes that some of her imaginative bent was due to her
father's being an actor. The walls of their bedroom were covered with
children's books. Her father used to read Dickens. 'I used to get up
and look at these books before I could read.' Joy used to pretend to
read aloud. During holidays, she and her sister would lie in bed all
day and 'read and read. I liked to do all the funny voices'. She couldn't
remember what books she didn't like as a child 'because I never read
them'. As a theatrical family, they valued freedom and doing what
you wanted. Their parents talked freely to them, 'perhaps too much
for our own good at times'. Fairyland was quiet, it seems, by
comparison with the real home.

LEONORA – PLAYING ORPHANS

When Leonora was about 7 or 8, she and two of her friends started
The Game, which they played for some years whenever they were able
to get together. They brought it to an end only when, at the onset
of adolescence, they began to feel self-conscious about it.

The Game's setting was an orphanage, 'a boarding establishment
run by a particularly vicious couple'. Leonora thinks the wife may
have been modelled on a 'narrow-minded religious woman' who had
had charge of her family during her mother's temporary absence. The
orphanage setting may have been inspired by 'the horrible tales of life
in an RC boarding school' told to one of the three girls by an Irish
domestic help.

The three girls were inmates in the orphanage, the terrifying warden
and his wife being the central imaginary characters. The Game was
the inventing and acting-out of incidents in the life of the orphanage,
but these incidents had to be plausible. The Game

> was frequently interrupted for an ongoing discussion of our actions,
> e.g., 'No, you can't possibly do that, it wouldn't be possible in the
> circumstances'. . . . Injustice was a strong concept in our Game.
> Why *should* people have to put up with certain treatments?

The Game, though exclusive to its three players (one girl dropped out,
but was replaced by another), was not secret: if their parents knew

about it, they just left them to get on with it, not interfering in any way.

Leonora thinks, in retrospect, that the satisfactions which it gave them were 'to do with creating a difficult challenge to be overcome. Basically [we] all had pretty easy childhoods; we enjoyed ourselves, our parents were OK, but we enjoyed beating the "them" in Our Game.'

She describes herself as having been a dreamy and scatterbrained little girl whom outsiders may have thought over-serious; 'but that's just the way I was/am, for God's sake!' She could read at 3½ and from then on, she was an omnivorous reader. Looking back, she recalls fantasies in which she delivered 'devastating punch-lines in recurring arguments', but she doesn't recall much self-doubt, nor feeling the need for withdrawal from the real world, though, she says, 'by implication, that was what The Game did for me/us'.

Many of the imagined incidents of 'The Game' were acted out by the participants, a practice which is common among young 'paracosmists'. The proceedings were frequently interrupted for discussions about how plausible they were.

No theory of the imagination is sufficiently comprehensive to explain why, as they get older, children worry about whether a fantasy is real enough. Is it boredom? Or do children become embarrassed because they start to judge what their imagination produces with what they have been taught to recognize as truly imaginative?

GEORGINA – RIDING SCHOOL

Georgina was a 'paracosmist' for a relatively short period in her childhood, between the ages of about 8 and 10. She and her friend Hilda 'disliked the pointlessness of life without something [to] make up for disappointments'. Their response to this challenge was to create an imaginary riding school. Their choice of this particular form of fantasy owed a great deal to their admiration of Hilda's elder sister Susan, an accomplished horsewoman whom the younger girls used to think of as 'Pat Smythe'. Susan helped the little girls by teaching them horsemanship (their 'horse' was a particular tree), giving them worn-out dandy brushes and tack to play with, and showing them how to use it. 'I used to imagine that I was training for such events as the Horse of the Year Show. . . . If it was wet, Hilda and I would "ride" indoors, sitting back-to-front on chairs.'

There was nothing secret about this private world; other children shared in it, and their parents took a benevolent interest. When she was away from home, Georgina would read everything she could lay her hands on to do with horses. She appears to have been a quite normal, healthy little girl, light-hearted and self-confident. She had three brothers and hers was a close-knit family. It was not a particularly cultured family – their daily paper was the *Daily Express* – but it was not authoritarian. Georgina enjoyed her school-days on the whole, but she attributes this in large measure to her own efforts; 'life is what you make it. . . . I didn't have very many friends at school as I considered myself the Faithful sort, and I didn't approve of fickleness (and I still don't).' She records that her childhood was 'happy enough. Even during bad times, nobody could suspect that my private world was helping cheer me up and get me over them.'

For Georgina more than with others, the fantasy would appear to have been a cure or compensation for boredom and disappointment. According to Freud, fascination with animals like horses is a sign of interest in sexuality in girls before puberty. Acting out running a riding school might be a clever, unconscious way of exploring that interest. Certainly if it was, the little girls didn't know it, but fantasy worlds can fulfil needs you never knew you had.

JIM – OR CAN A HOUSING PROBLEM CREATE A FANTASY WORLD?

Jim's imaginary world is unique among the cases we have encountered: it was a theatre. He cannot remember a time when he was not keen on the theatre but 'the private world entity came into being' when he was about 9. It did not wear off so much as merge into reality 'give or take a few disappointments'. He lived out his fantasy. His life has been bound up with the drama, as actor, producer, teacher, and playwright for the stage and broadcasting.

His imaginary theatre was entirely cerebral. Jim wrote down virtually nothing, made no models and drew no designs. Maps and plans were not necessary. 'It was set in the here-and-now . . . and was almost entirely interior. There might have been an occasional glimpse outside, but that did not interest me.' He was concerned with both 'back stage' and 'front-of-house', with mentally designing and building sets, choosing the plays for his imaginary company of players, casting, and finally producing them. He would identify with all his actors, none of whom was based on people he knew.

This private world was a spontaneous creation, inspired by his visits to the local Theatre Royal and to any other theatres he could get to. It was real for him: 'I think I was born with an instinctual conception of the disciplines of the drama.' It was a solitary pursuit, secret not so much because he wanted to protect it, as because no one else would have been interested. He loved inventing stories about the theatre and in it, though he rarely wrote anything. Somewhat flamboyantly, perhaps, Jim argues, 'The whole thing was entirely imaginary – a state of creative purity to which I aspire to return'.

He was completely single-minded in his devotion to the theatre, having no other hobbies which might have found their way in. He would 'diligently research the worlds of Zenda, Hentzau and Ruritania; but didn't want to know about Baldwin or Ramsay MacDonald'. Jim's private world was 'the kind of escapism judiciously necessary to keep people sane'. He sees it as having provided him with a way of withdrawing from the real world in which he felt, often unpredictably, controlled. But he was good at opting out, anyway.

Jim is, he claims, and always has been, 'an incurable romantic'. His definition of romance is sweeping as it includes 'beauty, miracle, panache, altruism, devotion, faith, gesture as significant, the reality of symbol, the creative quality of agony and the ultimate triumph of blessing over curse. (All in fact religious qualities).' Not much left out either! But, he continues,

> I would probably not have gone to the trouble of calling upon my imagination to set up a private world if I had not had a particular reality to escape from, and one in which the struggle for the romantic was in one sense directly involved. This was the lack in our household of any physical privacy.

More than with most, Jim needed to be able to opt out. Seven people – with odd extras at time of crisis – were crammed into a four-room house. He was given a room, and a bed, to share with Cousin Liz. 'One could be absolutely alone only in the loo out in the back yard.' He shuttered Liz out as a human being. He remembers reading *Lorna Doone* and Liz 'lying alongside trying to sleep. Lorna Doone was the human being. Poor Liz was a tedious, non-personal encumbrance grumbling about keeping the light on.' He couldn't feel romantic to her 'but our stark accessibility on the physical level – which I must then have sensed to be hostile to the proper business of romance – was a continuing hazard'. She pushed him both into the fantasy theatre and, eventually, into the real theatre.

Jim sees himself as having been a dreamy and imaginative boy; easy-going, but conscientious and reliable; tender-minded; bad at games; unmechanically minded; solitary and very single-minded. He was an early reader; at the age of 9 he stumbled upon *Adam Bede* which, though he could not fully understand it, 'pleasurably haunted' him for some time. Except for the *Children's Encyclopaedia*, 'which gave me most of my education', there were few books in his 'relaxed working-class home'. The radio was on continuously, though at the first bars of any chamber music, 'there was a concerted rush to switch it off. . . . Cultural interests were discouraged, as being beyond our station, unless it was apparent that they might help one to "get on" (i.e. to get a job in an office).'

Despite the crowding, the family got on well together and at times of need they helped each other. They appreciated 'honesty, thrift, truth-telling, respectability, and caring for others (as long as this wasn't a big production number!)'. Shiftlessness, untidiness, recklessness, and excess of any kind were frowned on. Religion meant 'behaving oneself'; Grandmother's membership of the Plymouth Brethren had no effect on the family life, except for making them feel they had to avoid hurting the old lady's feelings. Jim's theatre wasn't called The Globe!

Discipline was authoritarian, but Jim did not resent this. Uninhibited discussion with his parents was impossible, and, though he wasn't taken into their confidence, he didn't particularly want to be. His moments of greatest happiness in childhood were in 'reading, dreaming, acting, and watching plays and films'. He hated 'sports, anything to do with maths or science, parties and shopping'. He vividly recalls having the ability, as a child, to view himself with detachment though he never seems to have been detached about his crush on romance. He wanted outside support for his conviction that 'romantic living was valid'. On balance, he says, his childhood was a happy one. His imaginary theatre gave him 'a high degree of fantasy-indulgence, and the satisfaction of hope (that all is not lost) and faith (that all is not sour)!'

VERONICA - HEROINES ALL

Veronica was about 10 when she and her younger sister created an imaginary school. It enthralled them both for the next two years. It was inspired by a book of school stories which figured two heroic school-girls; Veronica and her sister created their own two heroines, and identified with them. 'We spent hours writing school magazines but no one else knew about this private world.' Recalling it, Veronica offered an automatic psychological motive for the fantasy:

> In actual life I was frightened by my school and simply loathed it, especially any form of sports or gymnastics. In our private world we were the Head Mistress's right-hand women, and were always finding the gym mistress (based on our real one) in compromising situations. We won all the prizes; edited the magazine; saved the exam papers from being opened by the sneak in the Fourth; captained the hockey team; and were generally as successful as the two girls in the prototype. We did have a scapegoat, however, and she was always, together with the gym mistress, being compromised and made to look a fool. . . . I think we were largely acting out our own real fears. . . . By making the greatest object of our fear, the gym mistress, into a ridiculous character, I think I might have put the school into better perspective.

The principal satisfaction which, Veronica says, she derived from this world was

> in getting some measure of control over the people who were making my own real school-days such a misery, and substituting someone else in my own real role as the unsuccessful under-achiever. By humiliating those who humiliated me (and we really did write some dreadful things about some members of the staff in the magazine) I suppose we hit back at authority in the only way we knew. . . . I think it was sheer wish-fulfilment.

In retrospect, Veronica wonders whether the fact that, as a child, she could see herself only utterly subjectively lay behind her need for a private world.

At the time Veronica was an apprehensive, imaginative, and reliable child, bad at games, 'adventurous within the family circle but not outside it: energetic and self-confident at home, though not at school. . . . I loved books where real people and real-life situations were involved. . . . I hated myths and legends.' She fantasized a good deal, but they were not fantasies of aggression. 'To the outside world I presented a lively, rather bossy, self-confident face. I think probably the two different Me's, of school and of home, required a fantasy world to bridge the gap.'

45

There were five children in Veronica's family. Her happiest childhood memories include being at home in the holidays and, as the eldest, organizing the family in imaginative play. Her parents were socialist and her mother an Anglo-Catholic: they cultivated an unconventional progressive life-style 'with emphasis on healthy diets, bare feet, fresh-air and culture (especially music). . . . But looking back I see that success in conventional forms was important and that from the start I felt myself to lack the conventional marks of the successful.'

She was free to discuss anything with her parents, 'but I never discussed my *real* problems. They were too deep and were too shameful.' Nevertheless, her childhood at home was very happy; school was another matter. She did not get on well with her peers: 'I was shy and embarrassed, and felt that I was never accepted by them.'

If you recall your fantasy, you pierce it by seeing it as having been something you created not for fun but for need. And, sometimes, it's just hard to remember what you did invent.

SONIA - GAPS IN THE MEMORY

Some of those who responded to the Silvey questionnaire sketched out fascinating worlds but left (or could recall) few details. Sonia was one of these.

When Sonia was 12 she created an imaginary village. She drew a map of it and prepared a list of its 282 residents, with all their occupations. She knew who was related to whom, and she also knew a great deal about the local school (she had herself just changed her school). She drew each member of the staff and listed the children in each class.

Sonia had a quite conscious motive in all this activity; it was to provide her with a realistic setting for stories she would tell herself at a time when she suffered recurrent asthma. If the asthma did not keep her in bed, it prevented her from playing with other children. Her imaginary world proved very effective; she became absorbed in the dramas of her characters – good practice for her later career as a teacher, and voluntary work in marriage counselling.

Sonia thinks she may have picked up the idea of the village from a favourite book (she was an omnivorous reader); but she kept her village to herself as a purely private world. Her preoccupation with it lasted for some time (though not as long as the 'paracosms' of some children). While it lasted it completely held her interest. Her family, devoutly Catholic but progressive, consisted of both parents, three daughters (one severely handicapped) and one son. Apart from her asthma, her childhood was happy and she got on well with her peers at school. She describes herself as a child as bright, curious, imaginative, and outgoing.

Sonia's secret imaginary village, started when she was 12, was a sophisticated creation. It was deliberately devised as a setting for the daytime continued stories, which she liked to tell herself. In these stories, the dramas between characters was of prime importance; but there is no mention of Sonia's identifying herself with any of them.

STELLA AND ANDREA – CONELAND

Stella has supplied us with information about three private worlds in which she participated as a child. When she was 7, she and a friend, Pamela, created the world of 'Marylin and Sylvia'. A year later she and a different friend, Andrea, a year younger than she, created 'Coneland', and four years later, when they were 12 and 11, they set up 'The Beacons'. Andrea sent in information about both these worlds.

'Marylin' was a projection of what Pamela would have liked to have been, and 'Sylvia' performed the same function for Stella. 'They were beautiful, with long black hair . . . wore slip-on silver shoes [and] beautiful clothes.' They were popular and talented, in all the ways which the two girls envied. 'Above all [they were] self-sacrificial and brave, carrying out all sorts of courageous exploits.' This fantasy had a precise setting in a village in Lancashire where Marylin and Sylvia attended Crocusfield College. Stella and Pamela were relentless in making stories about their creations, 'probably deriving from an addiction to Enid Blyton'. Dolls and dressing-up formed another important part of their activity.

'Coneland' had its origin in Andrea's interest in Nature, and particularly in conifers and cones. It had a strong mythical element. In Coneland there were hollowed-out giant cones in which you could both fly and live. Maps and family trees were prepared. Some of the place names have a clear Tolkien-ish ring to them, Morigamore, Riverside Dale, Rivelington, Denseling and Snowgill Isle (which is spelled Ilse on the map). A scale is provided suggesting that it was 300 miles from Rivelington to the Great Forae which was Conish for 'forest'. There was also a Cedardale Museum and The Rainbow Gardens.

Stella provided a drawing of an English girl and a Conish girl; these two looked much the same though the English one wore trousers. An important story concerned the felling of the *denes*. The denes were giant trees and there were only three of them in the Great Forae. They stood 600 feet tall and, not surprisingly, 'are the tallest trees in the world'. The men used to come with cranes and lorries to take down the denes. It took 3,000 men to chop them down and hollow them out for the soft mushy bark inside which was put in tins and was 'good Conish food'. The hollowed-out denes could be lived in or could fly. The picture of English girl and Conish girl shows a flying dene in the background which looks much like a missile.

The central characters were the Royal Family, King Cherry and Queen Fiona (also known as Mr and Mrs Hill) together with their many children. 'They owned quite a bit of land' but their life had its prosaic aspects for they would take children shopping on a Saturday morning, do gardening, and make New Year resolutions. The doings of the Royals were the girls' main preoccupation; as Andrea says, 'I don't remember thinking very much about the commoners.'

Stella also included a series of drawings of the Royal Family, a few of whom sported exotic names like Filomena and Daffony and Fuchsia. The Royals also had a flying dene with wheels which resembled a flying sausage. There were also drawings of the jewels like Elisabeth's gold 'braclit' (their spelling) and of various kinds of cones like the jewelled larch, the ruby pine and fire cone.

The last of these three private worlds grew out of a story which Stella or Andrea (or both) had invented. It concerned an eccentric millionaire who, greatly troubled about what to do with his money, asked his three beloved nieces to imagine how their 'dream Home' would be. They described it in detail and later, unbeknown to them, he had it built. They fell in love with it, went to live there and soon were joined by lots of their friends. 'I'm not sure', says Andrea, 'what kind of a community it was. It was certainly not a school (I could never have invented a dream-world about a boarding school as the very idea of such "concentration camps" appalled me). The girls lived in this wonderful residence in its beautiful surroundings, and most of them were very happy.' 'The Beacons' was set somewhere in England. Originally Andrea's father gave her some wooden dolls with ping-pong ball heads. She painted faces on them and needed a home for them. The Beacons was born. It started as a vague sort of institution but they never quite worked out what it was. The one certainty was that it wasn't an orphanage since the girls' parents were still alive. By the time the girls were 14, Stella had pinned it down to being a 'holiday camp', a theme which seems to have evolved. Stella's favourite character was Bossy, who was based on her own rebellious older sister. There was also a girl called Teresa who lived there and had a very cheeky parrot called Carolino. All the girls had long flowing hair. The Beacons had to be realistic so the girls had to be in by certain times and they were told off if they were naughty: 'We couldn't have believed in the girls if they weren't subject to discipline as we were.' But the girls were allowed to take part in sports even though Stella hated them. In her family, in reality, Stella was kept on a tight rein.

Andrea retains a vivid picture of The Beacons with its 'long, long driveway, lined with gas lamps' which had a particular fascination for her. It was contemporary; there were passing references to the famous pop stars of the period. The form of The Beacons tended to change as the girls got older; thus when it began there were dormitories, but later, single rooms, each with its own bathroom. The two girls told, and wrote, stories about The Beacons and its inhabitants, which included a male figure, Peter Tanaga, the lamplighter. He became a father-figure to the residents, and eventually 'inevitably' married one of them. Andrea says: 'In all my private worlds I could imagine what it would be like to be the particular characters, but I would never enter their world as myself. I could pull the strings only.' She also says that there was a clear distinction in her mind between her day-dreams and her private world. The girls' imaginings gradually became more realistic; magic receded and the need to be plausible increased, especially in The Beacons. None of the three worlds was secret, but adults did not interfere.

Andrea says: 'It was nice to feel that anything that happened in "The Beacons" could not hurt, or affect, me in any way as I did not exist in their world.' Her 'ultimate pleasure was in having created something.' Stella's chief satisfaction was 'the feeling of being in control; . . . the feeling of being able to use my imagination without this being judged, or imposed upon'. Andrea thinks that, whereas Coneland 'was mainly escapist', they used The Beacons to work out personal relationships.

Both girls felt themselves to be, to some extent, 'controlled', but perhaps as much by their own limitations as by authority. Neither girl suffered from unsatisfactory personal relationships at home. (The worst problem Andrea seemed to have was that she hated her own name, and insisted on being known by another for some time.)

In some respects the two were similar in temperament; both say they were dreamy, imaginative children and bad at games. Stella was an early and avid reader, but Andrea was held back by ill-health; later she showed special interest in nature books. Andrea admits that 'Coneland' was mainly escapist but she suggests that they used The Beacons to work out personal relationships. Less magic and more reality with age.

ERICA – CREATING A CRAB

Erica was the second of five children. Less than two years separated her from her elder sister with whom, as she reached 18, she had a love/hate relationship. Her brother and two other sisters are very much younger. 'I got on well with my father and mother. My elder sister was my only trial.' Her parents were 'broad-minded Catholics', both well educated and highly cultivated. They actively encouraged their children's interest in reading, music and other arts. For the first five years of her life Erica lived in Brazil; later she travelled widely on family holidays.

Even though Erica's childhood was very happy, there were times when she felt the need to be alone, and it was then that she developed her private world. At first there were just imaginary people, but by the time she was about 7, thanks to some extent to her reading of Tolkien, Rosemary Sutcliffe, and C.S. Lewis, 'countries' started to grow up around them. At this stage Erica would invent for each new country a new set of characters, which invariably included a young female heroine. In time a single country, Crab, crystallized out.

Then Erica became increasingly interested in its impersonal aspects, in its geography and geology, flora and fauna, etc. She would invent historical events for Crab, largely derived from British history. In time she began to feel the need for a continuous history but she does not seem to have invented one. When she started to learn French, Erica set about devising a Crabian language, but reluctantly, and with some sense of frustration, abandoned the attempt as too difficult. Her early 'paracosms' were mythical and fantastic. Later she felt the desire to be more naturalistic; she did not, however, feel this to be a constraint on her imagination.

For a very brief period, about the time the 'language experiment' was in progress, Erica co-opted a school-friend into the life of Crab. The partnership didn't work out. Apart from that, she kept her private world to herself. Her parents knew about it and took a benevolent attitude; but there did come a time when they began to have misgivings in case the amount of time Erica was spending on it might make her school-work suffer. This was in fact a period when Erica was finding life difficult, and in retrospect she feels that her paracosmic absorption was therapeutic.

The pleasure which Erica derived from her fantasy arose as much from the creating and elaborating of it as from telling herself stories about it. Looking back, she identifies the nature of her satisfactions as 'privacy, and a chance to be creative; to invent, imagine and channel what I had been reading and thinking into some definite form'. She is inclined to attribute to her paracosmic imagining the credit for her adult interest in geography and history.

Erica thinks she was a timid child, but bright, conscientious, imaginative, and reliable. She was quite good at games and mechanically minded. She was also tender-minded. She did not start to read particularly early, but became an avid reader. She 'loved books about magic – but not magic in everyday life which always seemed incongruous'. She got on well with her peers at the small comprehensive convent school to which her parents sent her. She has her parents to thank, she says, for her 'broader education'.

Once again, we end with a private world in the present, described by a paracosmist who is a child at the time of writing.

DICKIE

At 5 years old Dickie already had a private world which meant a great deal to him. His father undertook to put to the child our questions about it, and to write down his answers.

Q. How old were you when you first began to have any imaginary world? Is it your very own, or do you share it with someone else?

A. I really have got a farm. I was about 2. I go there at night. I walk or fly my kite.

Q. Do you make up stories about what happens in it? And do you do anything else about it, for instance, draw maps or make models of it?

A. I don't make up stories about it; but I am going to make maps and models of it.

Q. It must be fun, or you wouldn't do it. Can you give us some idea of what *makes* it fun?

A. What makes it fun? Things like Hallowe'en, when I stay up late and have a party, and the animals have a merry dance outside.

Q. What other sorts of things do you specially like doing? And what sort of things do you really hate?

A. Throwing pies in the cow's face. Fighting, and playing marbles. I've got a big motorbike. I hate having to get dressed.

His father added that, during a recent family holiday, Dickie's farm was being quite seriously discussed by a group of adults. Dickie was present; after a time he crept close to his father and whispered 'Tell them it isn't a *real* farm'. (Such clear differentiation between pretence and reality develops in children at a very early age. See Flavell *et al.* 1987.)

Dickie claims that his private world dates back to the age of 2. Even when questioned, he was only 5. Structured imagination can start early.

Chapter Three

ISLANDS, COUNTRIES, AND THEIR PEOPLES

The next set of 'paracosms' revolve around places. In a way, all these worlds require the child to create a special place but most of the last set were very local and specific – orphanages, riding schools, the posh Beacons where young ladies might prepare themselves for the ordeals of the social whirl and social world. Different fantasies are dominated by making up a country and then organizing it. This kind of systematic imagination is psychologically very curious. On the one hand, children are playing, fantasizing, imagining; on the other hand, the fantasy is very logical. Events in their world have to follow rules. It looks much more like work than play. Yet the children 'play' it and, as we shall see, can dread losing it.

JANE – (TWO-WORLD JANE)

Jane cannot remember a time when she did not exist in both a real and an imaginary world. 'One of my earliest recollections is of playing with my hands as if they were two separate people, male and female.' When she was about 6, lying in bed in her grandfather's house, she would gaze at the cracked ceiling and see that

> between the uneven lumps on the discoloured surface ran roads and rivers – a landscape that I populated and named. . . . Back at home, this world was quickly transferred to a landscape created by the curly patterns impressed on the seat of a plywood chair. Here too were roads and rivers and sites for buildings.

As her imagination outgrew the chair-seat, she began drawing maps of her world. When her father had taught her to read Ordnance Survey maps and relate them to her surroundings, map-making became an important element in her private world. Gradually her maps became more detailed and sophisticated, turning into town-plans and architects' blueprints. Finally she created a suburban town. It had schools and hospitals and was like the one she lived in. 'I became very interested in its social organization, designing housing developments, shops, schools, hospitals, etc., and even considering pedestrian flow and traffic control. I was surprised, years later, to hear architects and town-planners discussing ''my'' problems!' Jane was interested in the town as a whole rather than in specific bits – imagination on a half-grand scale.

Her private world was contemporary. It did not have any history or link with any existing country, nor did Jane have any conscious model for it, though she was much impressed by R.L. Stevenson's *The Land of Counterpane*. Jane's world changed over time but its principal inhabitants remained constant; they were the most important elements. The most dear and familiar to her were an imagined brother and two sisters (Jane was an only child); now she recognizes that they 'were aspects of my own personality'. At the time she didn't realize that. The brother was closely modelled on her cousin. 'When I confessed how I had used him during his childhood, he was amused and curiously pleased.' Other characters were based on school-friends or neighbours, but some were wholly imaginary. She gave some of them names suggestive of *Pilgrim's Progress*, which appealed to her; others had Biblical or Dickensian names though, unfortunately, in her replies Jane gave no examples. I like to think some were biblical-Dickensian – Moses Pickwick, or Rehoboam Copperfield.

All the drama and action took place in personal dramas. Jane imagined her world during the Second World War but this had no special influence. Her people led ordinary lives, frequently punctuated by journeys. Sometimes they invented or found 'strange objects such as a ring with a large stone in which anything desired could be seen as in a mirror'. Jane's world was plausible and consistent and, as she wanted it so, she was never conscious that this hampered her imagination. Her interest in her private world 'wore off at puberty by which time I became aware of the dangers of getting confused between reality and fantasy'.

Jane's world was intensely private. 'No adult or other child ever knew about it and its privacy was part of its charm and value. It was very precious to me, not to be shared, and only indulged in in solitude or at times of withdrawal, like chapel services.' She says that as a child she found it easy to stand outside of herself; she would often draw pictures of herself with her imaginary family, and surprise people by her ability to depict accurately her own back-view! She does not recall feelings of aggression so much as feelings of self-doubt. Her secret imaginative life reassured her because she felt at a loss or disadvantage in the real world.

Her family was religious. Paradoxically it was on Sundays that Jane found her world to be most important to her. In her teens she would withdraw into the suburban town. Her expression would be blank but she was 'inwardly absorbed' by the doings of the town. She never found a child to share it with and thought the Brontës were 'lucky' to share their imaginings. She never seems to have experienced a need to finalize her world on paper. Only on a few occasions did she write letters between members of her family or draw portraits of them.

I enjoyed reading, drawing and painting, acting, being in the countryside especially with animals of any kind . . . above all to be in the company of any one loved and trusted person with whom I felt some true rapport (adult or child). I hated to be made to do anything in public e.g. going to a party (acting was different), making polite conversation, wearing formal girl's clothing especially hats, and being involved in any kind of religious occasion. (I desperately wished I had been born a boy.)

Yet, the stories she liked best had religious overtones; they were legends and Norse myths.

Because of ill-health, Jane did not go to school until she was 8. She found it hard to adjust till she got to secondary school. At about 13, she made one firm and lasting friendship which changed her life in many ways and led to other friendships. It coincided with her losing interest in her private world.

The satisfactions which she derived from it were

enormous, continuing and felt in many ways. It provided company, interesting variety, freedom (when confined to bed or to the chapel pew), and possibly a sense of power to control something which I was too timid to attempt in reality . . . . I used my private world as an escape from boredom, loneliness and an embarrassing shyness, and as an entertainment which could take place anywhere.

Jane used it to withdraw from a slightly oppressive real world.

It was a substitute for personal relationships, for I was isolated by my somewhat snobbish, extremely religious family and by my poor health. . . . I was always fascinated by people. I think my private world was a way of examining personal relationships.

That sounds a little grand perhaps, or the kind of thing one says looking back to justify what might look to others a bit frivolous and silly.

BERYL – MOHAWKS AND WOLVES

'I think I was about 5 . . . when I first created my private world. My interest probably reached its zenith between the ages of 9 and 16, and began to dwindle gradually.' It was an island which expanded considerably over the years, though its basic shape and form never changed. It was on this planet, but its precise location was both vague and irrelevant, for it had no structure, no government and no relations with the outside world. 'I was not at all interested in its history but extremely particular about its geography and natural features.'

Writing in the present tense, for the island is still vivid in her mind after sixty years, Beryl says: 'The west coast is rather like Orkney, with high cliffs which tail off to the south where the coastline remains rocky.' There are one or two tall stacks like the Old Man of Hoy, palm trees and an abundance of excellent sea-food. Crabs and clams, lobsters and mussels paddled off-shore, though Beryl was too young to provide her island with restaurants. The south coast was almost tropical, with gorgeous beaches of white sand where turtles came to lay their eggs. On the east coast, a splendidly wide estuary teemed with sea-birds and waders. There were sand dunes and rocky inlets where seals bred and terns nested. Inland there were high mountains. The north-west had wide plains where buffalo and antelope roamed, preyed on by a pack of semi-tame wolves led by Akela, who had been transported from Kipling's *Jungle Book*. There was also a tract called Mohawk Country where there were Indians and herds of wild horses. 'There were rolling grassy foothills to the north, and beyond them a phantasy land, peopled by fauns and dryads and the Great God Pan (down in the reeds by the river). I have also seen and stroked a unicorn there', Beryl noted. There were pine forests up in the north-west, but further south the trees were deciduous.

Beryl lived in a log hut with a wolf-dog, Lobo, and she travelled around on an Arab mare called Hadvor.

56

These two have been my constant companions since I was about 7, but they never seem to get any older. I also had a magic boat in my youth for a while. It had an out-board motor but I found that too noisy. I've never been clever with engines and there were always problems about petrol, so I discarded the idea!

She had, successively, Mowgli, Peter Pan, and Tarzan (without the apes) as companions, and also a Greek boy called Hermes; but as she grew older, they each moved away. 'I never actually banished anyone, though. They simply moved . . . to a different part of the island and I visited them less often.' Imaginary characters and animals played quite a large part, but 'I don't think I ever identified with any of them. They were simply my friends.'

They used to hold Olympic Games on the island, and have wrestling and shooting matches and swimming and diving contests, and show-off feats of horsemanship. Orpheus and Apollo were among the inhabitants or visitors to the north shore, so they provided wonderful music. Beryl invented all sorts of adventures and stories and acted them out. But they all had to be logical and natural. Both on her island, and in her real childhood, Beryl loved swimming and riding, especially riding bare back on the beach.

Beryl's 'paracosm' was not merely private but totally secret: 'I went to a great deal of trouble to keep it to myself.' Looking back, she does not find it easy to identify the nature of the 'enormous and lasting' satisfactions which she derived from it. It was not an escape from difficult human relationships, of which she was singularly free. 'I was very fond of my parents and guardians', and of her only brother who was younger.

Beryl outwardly accepted discipline but noted wryly: 'At a very early age, I lost my faith in the infallibility of my elders.' She was 4 when her brother was born and her mother told her 'an angel had brought him. My grandmother said it was a stork.' The maid said the doctor had brought him in his black bag while the cook said that he was found under a gooseberry bush. Were there different ways of babies arriving? No, said the grown ups. When she was 7, Beryl consulted the encyclopaedia and learned the truth. Three months after her brother's birth, Beryl was taken Christmas shopping. All the department stores in Edinburgh had a Father Christmas. 'On the way home, I enquired if there was more than one Father Christmas. And was told no. And that finished me. From then on I didn't believe a word grown ups said.' And she determined to keep her private world very private.

She thinks it may have been that it was only in solitary imaginative play that she could fully express herself. Other children's imaginations seemed to her very limited. 'My secret world was different, and far, far better.' In it, she was able to give vicarious expression to all those many pursuits – from riding to bird-watching – which meant so much to her.

Beryl was an early and omnivorous reader. She disliked *Alice*, and was thoroughly frightened by *Struwwelpeter* and by some of Grimms' tales. But she loved the *Jungle Books*, *Puck of Pook's Hill*, *Rewards and Fairies*, and the works of E. Nesbit and Robert Louis Stevenson. At 11 she started to collect Wells's *History of the World*, then being published in fortnightly parts. As a teenager she read Darwin's *Origin of Species* and *The Ascent of Man*. She was 'steeped in poetry from a very early age', and was particularly interested in myths and legends.

MIRIAM AND MARGARET – THE GREAT DICTATOR

Miriam has long been a successful novelist and writer of stories for children. When she was about 8 or 9 she and her younger brother created a race called the Minaturians. They were very small people, so small that, for them, cart ruts were streets. There was a Minaturian Magazine which Miriam edited and illustrated; 'Daddy read it with great amusement'.

By the age of 11, Miriam had dropped the Minaturians. With a friend called Margaret, she embarked on a new world. It started 'as an island which I drew; my friend Margaret also drawing an island of her own'. They at once invented, and drew, the royal families and from then on the islands' 'game' developed. Miriam had the east side and Margaret the west. The rest of the world evolved from enemy countries they invented, the best and most vivid of which was Margaret's, Urilla, an unpleasant dictatorship. From the first, the shape of the island was fixed; fifty years on, Miriam could still sketch it.

Insulo and Prosperito – 'pronounced Prosperorighto' – were on another planet which wasn't necessarily in our solar system. The girls called it Dionysus because they were learning Greek and loved it. At the time when Miriam originally created Insula she was 'mad about Nordic Gods and heroes and also on Latin, so that many place-names were bogus Nordic or Latin. . . Later I worked out more English-sounding names for the various provinces, towns and villages.' At first their world was historical.

The original royal families wore tunics . . . but later we made up a lot of people in 'modern' times [the 1930s]. After we had explored two generations ahead, the 1970s seemed unreal; so we shunted them all back 100 years into the Napoleonic period.

There were Earls and Lords, 'some nice, some nasty. In time, the royal family became progressively nicer.' As well as maps, there were 'notebooks of historical dates, dynasties, wars, major writers with titles of plays etc. (Insula had a Shakespeare called Odin Peerwell), legends, orders of chivalry and patron saints'. At the end of the eighteenth century Queen Elfrida of Insula married Prosperito's greatest general, 'thereby causing a lot of confusion in the Insulan succession'. Insulans and Prosperitans spoke related languages though the girls did not work out their languages for them. 'Prosperito had a slightly French atmosphere (many kings called Louis), but the country was rather like Scotland. . . . Insula got more and more English. Urilia, our enemy country, was, I regret to say, rather Germanic.' However, Urilia's dictator, Vanderan, resembled Mussolini rather than Hitler. He, too, became more like Napoleon when they shifted their world back in time. (It's not clear why Miriam said Vanderan was more like Mussolini.) Both 'now' and 'then', Vanderan's Nazi-style secret police persecuted the Yaronites, an amalgam of Jews and gypsies who had, however, a homeland which Urilia had overrun. 'Some of my favourite heroes were Yaronites. They were tremendously musical.' Miriam realized they were mimicking contemporary events.

At first, the islands were wracked with disasters, earthquakes, floods, and hurricanes. The villains were 'diabolically cunning'. As the world gelled, it became more realistic

though always very romantic, of course. Our people were not children but grown ups, leading adventurous lives with love affairs to match. We got interested in the love affairs a bit later than the adventures, but they soon became important. . . . The people were the most important part of our world. . . . It was our soap-opera I suppose.

The girls did not identify with their characters: 'they were like the characters a novelist uses'. At first, they talked in the characters of their people and Miriam thinks this may be why she started out her career as an author by writing plays. Eventually they had three main heroes who were always adventuring and conquering 'villainous groups'. Miriam thinks that these adventures could have been imagined quite easily on Earth but they felt freer to create earthquakes and floods on the planet Dionysus. In their mid-teens the fantasy blossomed. There were three generations of characters. Miriam wrote a 400-page novel about the pseudo-Napoleonic wars they made up. The adventures were grisly, full of tortures and wounds which are 'typical aggression features'. She wasn't conscious of using the world to work out problems or to express her self-doubts though her characters often 'could do well what I could only do badly'. Miriam loved music and had a good ear, but was never a good pianist: 'I consequently made up people who were proficient.'

> Our writing (about our private world) began with War Reports. We then went on to writing bits of people's letters and then scenes. We generally wrote separately and read each other's, though we did do one or two stories together – both making it up, but each writing it down in turn.

They would also tell one another stories about their world when on country walks or at home in winter. This joint enterprise continued well into their adolescence, reaching a peak when they were 15–17. They became more secretive as they grew older. Miriam added: 'I used to worry because I couldn't make up people in the real world but always had to latch them on to the Insulan families which had become so real to me.'

Their private world was not secret, but nobody joined in the making up. Their families knew about it and were perhaps 'somewhat puzzled by our obsession with it'. Miriam still made up imaginary games with her brother as she got older. Insula outlasted any of these, which included games based on *Swallows and Amazons*. While Miriam does not feel her fantasy was any particular encouragement to the 'ferreting-out' of facts, 'It may have helped one to sort out one's ideas about people and life. I tried out various life-styles vicariously, as it were.'

If Insula did not represent for her an escape from a controlled environment, she feels she was lucky because she never wanted to opt out. Miriam's father died when she was 11 and the family moved from the country into a town. The islands may have been compensations for both these losses. The satisfaction which it brought her 'was essentially the same as I now get from writing novels . . . though how one defines the pleasure of the imagination, I don't know!' Miriam was a bright child, rather shy and easily over-excited as a little girl. She had 'many friends but liked to be alone a lot'. Miriam felt: 'I was inside myself so much that it was years before I discovered other people did not feel or react just as I did.' She was eager to learn about a lot of things. She hated competitive games, ball-games in particular, because she was short-sighted. Hers was a home in which books were plentiful and she learned to read early. As a little girl she disliked Hans Christian Andersen because 'there was too much unhappiness': she preferred the Brothers Grimm. In her teens her favourite author was Jane Austen. Neither radio nor the cinema 'influenced our saga much'.

Her greatest pleasures in childhood included 'going to the sea and bathing . . . imaginative games . . . drawing and painting, writing poems and (later) our world'. Her hates included meeting strangers, 'but when they turned out to be friends, it was marvellous'. Hers was a happy childhood.

Miriam's fellow fantasist describes a similar world but for her whatever she happened to be interested in at any particular moment found expression in her paracosm. The two girls appear to have had many common characteristics as children. Both were highly imaginative, both (vicariously) adventurous, but bad at games; neither was given to self-examination nor had fantasies of aggression; both were keen readers; both quite enjoyed their school-days and got on reasonably well with their peers.

Margaret makes the point that since both girls led sheltered (and happy) lives as children, their private world gave them 'the chance to have adventures and experiences that we could not have had and, indeed, were not ready for. . . . In fact I think it was when things really happened to US that the thing started to fade.' It gave her the same pleasure as reading books 'with the added satisfaction that our people sometimes took things into their own hands, and also [Miriam's] reactions with her people made it a game of give and take with surprises. . . . Possibly . . . when we got to the stage of talking romances' (by which time they were well into their teens), 'we got some vicarious sexual satisfaction; but this was never physical – always in the imagination'.

Miriam eventually published a book which was inspired by this world – one of the few examples of a 'practical' result from all this fantasy.

DAVID – BURROWING TO BEARLAND

David shared the imaginary private world of Bearland with his elder brother Peter. They were the children of Gerald, who in childhood had had his own fantasy of Chlorophilia. Their father, however, doubts very much whether, at the time of the creation of Bearland, either of them knew anything about his world.

Peter spontaneously created Bearland when he was about 10. David, who is our reporter, describes its beginnings as 'a loose community of stuffed animals, mainly bears, and other creatures on a peripheral basis e.g. hamsters, mice and occasionally human beings, and a few imaginary characters'. Peter, as the elder, was the main driving force; David, four years younger, felt that Bearland had 'always been there. . . . It changed and developed over the years with both of us taking initiatives in its evolution. . . . We had no literary or visual model, it just seemed to develop between us.'

Bearland had a complex history. It had a legendary past, and a contemporary history built up as things happened and recorded in state documents. The documents started in 1949 before they were born. There was a written history book, and Bearland's natural history was also written. There were one-inch-to-the-mile maps of the most populous districts, which fitted into a global longitude and latitude grid system. 'The bears lived in our playroom and activity was assumed to go on in our absence. . . . They were the central characters and round them all the components revolved.' David, as the younger, felt both that this parallel world was always there and that it grew out of their own games. They had their own fully formed characters and roles, such as kings, citizens, prime ministers, crooks, teachers, etc., which might vary over the years. 'The hamsters stayed in their cages, and history was written for them without their actually taking part.'

There was a written code of Playroom Rules, of which *Paragraph 0:11* read: 'There is no blaming things on to the bears, they are only alive to a certain extent.' Peter would sometimes turn down his younger brother's suggestions with 'You can't do that, it isn't allowed'. Peter invented a Bearean language into which he translated the Bearean Bible, later producing a textbook entitled 'Modern Bearean'. It looked much like Greek with a few extra rune-like letters. Peter was about 14 when he made this up and it was the high-point of his involvement. The language had its own script which David, to this day, has never

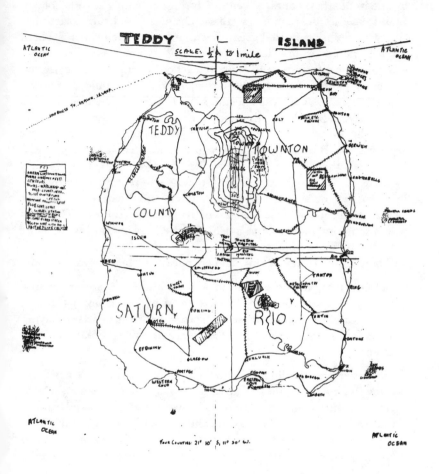

An example of an invented island

63

managed to master. When addressing the bears you had to speak in a falsetto voice.

Events in the outside world, or in the family, often triggered off events in Bearland. Thus a British general election would be followed by one in Bearland, or an adventure during the family seaside holiday would have its Bearean counterpart. Dramas could turn gruesome. 'We sometimes conducted grisly executions of plasticine men.' There was a certain division of labour between the two brothers; Peter, who was more academic, would write the school curricula or devise the monetary system. David, who was more artistic, would design the banknotes, paint the Court pictures, and decorate the tombs. Both boys made the models with which they fleshed out the world.

All the boys' interests, passing or permanent, tended to find expression in Bearland: 'It lived with us and was part of our lives.' David feels that, in the day-to-day life, the two elements – creating the structure of Bearland and story-telling – were equally enjoyable. In retrospect he sees their preoccupation with Bearland as having helped them cope with the business of living in the real world. Perhaps it was sometimes an 'escape-hatch'; but he is sure that for the most part it was 'sheer enjoyment'.

Their parents knew about, and encouraged, their private worlds,

> helping us to plan documents to be more authentic, and suggesting things the bears could do. We told them what was going on. . . .
> A friend of my brother at school started his own Bearland having been introduced to ours, and his bears sometimes took part in our events.

While Peter was the linguist, David was more visual. When Peter became less interested after completing the Bearean translations, David became the main fantasist. He transformed Bearland into a Regency world, with early steam locomotives and towns full of Adam buildings.

Theirs was a happy family, but it had its hidden tensions. David thinks Bearland made them less insecure. He has no doubt about the pleasure he derived from it:

> It was the same as I now derive from painting – that of creativity. Additionally, it provided imaginary friends in a small family world. I had friends at school, but the family was the only real close contact I had with other people.

Though a late reader, he became a voracious one. He loved myths and legends, all fantasy and stories involving magic. His personal fantasy life was very vivid. At 8 he was quite convinced that the box-room door of their flat opened on to hidden delights. He felt a real sense of loss when, eventually opening it, he discovered the truth. Television did not have much impact on him and he was seldom taken to the cinema. Radio, however, did have repercussions on Bearland which had its beat groups at the time when the Beatles and the Rolling Stones were in their heyday!

The family was close-knit, Peter being rather closer to his father and David to his mother. Gerald's scientific background encouraged both boys to try to discover for themselves how things worked, and their mother's painting influenced David's artistic propensities. They took the magazine *The Studio*. Books were both read and talked about. 'Painters visited and were visited. . . . The appreciation of good things, visual and literary, was encouraged.'

It was a liberal home. They were never beaten. Nevertheless, David remembers 'unreasoning fear and distrust sometimes overcame me, as when I was too scared to tell anyone that I had broken the bath-plug chain'. He did not feel that he could discuss everything with his parents.

The experiences he most enjoyed as a child were 'being in the country, being with my mother, seeing my uncle, going to interesting places with my dad. I hated school . . . and being alone in our flat, though I didn't mind if I knew my mother was around.' He feels that he got little out of school life 'except a hatred of wasting my time under other people's control and of institutions of all kinds'. While he had a number of school-friends, he always felt intimidated by most of his school-fellows. He sums up his childhood years as 'happy at home, hateful at school'.

DENIS – THE RAILWAY THAT SPANNED THE GLOBE

Denis created two distinct private worlds. The first, when he was 11, was an international railway system. But long before this, drawing people had been his obsession. He built up a gallery of individual people to whom he gave names and characters. Among them were a father and son, Dick and Dan Gerrard, 'who had been sacked from the LNER and given an old railway engine as a parting gift'. Together they laid a track, got some carriages, and started their railway. They prospered mightily. Their next move was to build a Channel tunnel and then an Atlantic tunnel. These feats were followed by a series of tunnels linking the East Indies from Singapore to Darwin – a phenomenal piece of engineering, after which came a multispan bridge from Sydney to Wellington. Denis nowhere comments on the sheer scale of all this. 'The *incidentals* to all this were', he notes, rail routes and stations throughout the world. It was possible to take the crack train from Vancouver to Wellington via New York, London (actually a station somewhere near Croydon, called Gerrard), and Sydney. Trains stopped at 'lesser places like Paris and Delhi on the way'. Denis placed the London station in Croydon so as not to conflict with 'real' London termini. 'Among the stations I provided was one at Verk-hoyansk in Siberia where the temperature extremes went from 85°F in the summer to – 40° in the winter.' Denis admitted that his engineering was less reliable that his map-reading, but 'I was rather proud of my tunnel building machine (laying the track behind it) and a very sophisticated engine which produced its own electricity as well as consuming it.'

Denis was not aware of any source for his railway though he was 'romantically attached' to trains. His school overlooked the line which carried the Paris boat train.

The Gerrards were not surprisingly ennobled, given their achievements in en-railing the world. Denis sent in a drawing of Dick, who became Viscount Gerrard of Gerrard and Atlantis. He looked like a much-whiskered dignitary.

Two years later, when Denis was 13, he was set off in a new direction by reading about Greyfriars School in *The Magnet*. He created his own imaginary school, calling it, improbably, St Thompsonn's, but he identified with the staff rather than with the pupils. All the teachers, and later all the governors, had a plethora of degrees, decorations, and later peerages. Eventually, Denis drew a personal peerage of fifty-six lords with potted biographies. Denis's hero was James Outridge, who was given a fake German identity and in reality owned a castle. Outridge resigned the Tory whip over Munich. Just as he could not bear to make his imaginary London station conflict with 'real' ones, Denis could not give any of his famous Thompsonnians real positions such as Prime Minister or Archbishop of Canterbury. He drew pictures of both, though, talking to the King but they seem to have been outside his imaginary world.

Denis's brother also drew but what was oddest was that his own imaginary world led to two emulations. A school-friend called Henry

invented a small school called St Martin's, which had only two staff.
A cousin devised an imaginary country called Coronan.

A surviving book of portraits gives 134 separate men, each with
head and shoulders, full names, decorations, titles, dates of birth
and potted biography, school, university etc. Most had no life
beyond the initial act of creation, but a few were my constant
companions. I identified to a limited extent. I *was* each person as
I drew him and imagined him speaking and acting, but I think I
was always totally outside them. They were my characters, but I
do not think I was ever identifying with them, except when I had
a pencil in my hand.

Since it was important to Denis that he should 'retain his own
credibility', he found that all this activity involved him in a great deal
of research in *Whitaker's Almanac, Burke's Peerage,* and the like, and on
medals and decorations. It offered 'total absorption in a world richer
than my own. I was creating, and in a sense being, a large number
of high-achieving, distinguished, dignified men.' He escaped into an
adult and high-powered world. Did it also bring creative satisfaction?

I enjoyed drawing and being able to do something some others said
they could not do. The drawings were not as good as I thought they
were at the time, but they served my purpose.

He learned about medals, titles, heraldry, uniforms, and historical
sites. All his characters were men and many were military. Denis claims
the fantasy allowed him to be snobbish and hang on to more socialist
ideals but it's hard to see just where the socialist ideals fitted in. To
give an example of the elaboration of titles, Outridge began as Col.
Sir James, and eventually Denis's world was peopled by such as the
1st Duke of Strathcoombe and Janipur and others of that ilk. 'I enjoyed
the useless knowledge aspect – I was a quiz kid.'

There was nothing secret about either of Denis's worlds. Both his
parents and his only sibling – a much adored elder brother – all took
a benevolent attitude to them. His involvement in both finally died
away when he was about 14.

He says that he was an imaginative and curious child, but lethargic
and bad at games. By contrast, the characters he created were not
only male, but uniformly masterly, if not martial. His family were
politically aware. Sex was 'obviously unmentionable. Conservatives
were as wicked as sex – more so because we talked about them.'

Once again we end the chapter with a current private world.

SEAN AND DOUGLAS

Sean and Douglas, both aged 13, are near-neighbours and very close friends, though they go to different schools. They have imaginary countries, Awentishland and Rull respectively, and continue to be absorbed in them. Awentishland and Rull are adjacent states whose relationship historically resembles that of England and Scotland. Even though they are on another planet, they could be on Earth. Both countries have histories much like that of Europe, for example they were involved in 'Great Wars' in the periods 1914–18 and 1939–45. (The enemy in each case was a group of 'Communist' powers which were duly vanquished.)

Both states are limited monarchies with parliamentary systems of government. In Awentishland the two major political parties alternate in office fairly regularly though what political principles divide them is obscure. (The names of the parties offer no clue.)

The main source of information about both these states is a 16,000-word manuscript in Sean's hand, entitled 'A History of Awentishland: 158 pp of truthful facts'. The date of publication is given as 1980 and the retail price as £1.00. While it is impossible not to be aware of the similarities of Awentish and English history, there are differences. Awentishland was converted from paganism to Christianity in AD 833 but has its Pope, who is elected by the natives. Apparently the Reformation did not touch Awentishland. (Sean's is a practising Catholic family.)

Neither is Rull a slavish copy of any existing state. Douglas writes:

> I find that my ideals for the UK come to life in Rull. For instance, I believe there should be no private motor cars. There should be massive gardens and Victorian houses for everyone; no nuclear power; there should be many trees and bicycles. . . . Oh! Yes; most important; no weapons or killing!

Later Douglas tells us of the two most recent Acts to reach the Rull Statute Book: one requires everyone to plant a tree every day, the other bans the name David. Existing Davids must change their names. No explanation of this law is given.

Both boys are football enthusiasts; they found it necessary between them to create enough imaginary countries to justify competition for a World Cup. Sean declares that he has written no fewer than twenty-two books about aspects of football in Awentishland, and that 'every week my friend Douglas rolls the dice, consults his charts, and comes out with extremely realistic football results'.

Neither Sean nor Douglas sees their private lands as an escape from difficult family circumstances. Who knows how their fantasy will evolve?

Chapter Four

SYSTEMS, DOCUMENTS, AND LANGUAGES

As children get older, they seem to divide into two different kinds. Some abandon their fantasy worlds altogether: it's too childish. Others, especially boys, seem to elaborate them, bringing in all kinds of details that mimic the real world. 'Paracosms' become vehicles for very specific interests such as the creation of special languages or elaborate political systems. What's striking about these is how, usually, they parallel the real world. Writers like Tolkien or Ursula Le Guin, who create veritable universes, go out of their way to make them different from ours. Tolkien's Middle Earth is one continent, with the sundering seas being the ultimate divide. Sail from the Grey Havens and you sail into the mists of time, memory, and outside the compass of the world. Le Guin's Earth Sea is the opposite of Middle Earth, a world of nothing but islands. The sea joins them instead of dividing. The children seem not to make these leaps into imagining very different worlds but to create something that is very close to what they know – embellishing it with passion and frenzy.

Robert Silvey's own world (see pp. 11–13) was very much of this literal sort. Before he died, he wrote an account of his own feelings about it and it seems a good way to begin these excerpts.

ROBERT

The New Hentian States was a federal republic occupying the whole of an island-continent, about six times as large as Great Britain. It was situated in the South Atlantic and, in the words of its brief history to be found in the 'Government Handbook for 1920', it had originally been discovered by a British frigate and 'found to be inhabited by a race of peaceful Indians'. In the sixteenth century it was colonized by a party of some 300 Dissenters and 100 Huguenots. In 1700 King William of England recognized its independence. In 1788, when the population had grown to over twelve million, the New Hentian States, having outgrown its existing constitution, was declared a federal republic, with a President as Chief Executive, a bi-cameral legislature and a Supreme Court.

I can trace the first stirrings of this form of imagining to a time before I could read, when I was fascinated by the family atlas. It is a short step from poring over maps to drawing imaginary ones of one's own.

There was soon no doubt in my mind that no self-respecting state could lack a Year Book, so, in the unused pages of a chemistry notebook I began, in the summer holidays of 1917, laboriously compiling one for the New Hentian States.

My private world was *not* one in which imaginary personalities and the play of character were of great importance. The private lives of Hentia's citizens were of no concern to me.

The actual process of creating the social, economic and political institutions gave me the same sort of pleasure, so I gathered, as other boys got from designing and constructing highly complicated models in Meccano – models which they would cheerfully demolish as soon as they were completed, since all the fun lay in the act of making.

The accommodating quality of a 'paracosm' could have strategic uses. Thus, in my non-conformist home sixty years ago, eyebrows were raised when I was found to be grappling with Hentian problems on the Lord's Day. But I was able to disarm all criticism by pointing out that I was busy organizing the religious life of my imaginary country!

It will be apparent that my 'paracosms', though private, were not secret. My family and some family friends knew about them. (When my own children reached the appropriate age, I told them about my private worlds: but though they seemed quite interested, the idea did not catch on with any of them: their imaginative lives took a different form.)

Somewhat about the age of 15, I remember, I told myself that I 'had better be careful or I would become more interested in my imaginary world than I was in reality', but the fact was that I was outgrowing my 'paracosm'; my absorption in it soon began to

71

wane, and I was conscious of gradually feeling an increasing detachment from it. Yet I never experienced a reaction from it, still less any adolescent shame about my 'childish' interests.

I was rather an over-sensitive boy, tender rather than tough-minded, with an enquiring and logical mind, quite intelligent but certainly not 'brilliant'. I was certainly highly imaginative, but I showed no exceptional artistic aptitudes. I was studious but not particularly ambitious. I was less than averagely gregarious, much preferring one close friend to a gang of acquaintances. To my great chagrin, I was quite hopeless at all ball-games and 'gym'. It may seem an absurd exaggeration to say that this is something which can mark a man for life, but nevertheless it is true. It was not until many years after I left school that I ceased to smart under a sense of unquestioned inferiority on this account. Amongst the generality of my school-fellows, I would have been regarded as without any standing whatever, were it not that I built up a modest reputation as a mimic and comedian in house concerts.

I do not think that I was a particularly early reader, but I was 'read to' a great deal. My father read many of the classics to the assembled family, and after his death, when I was ten, my elder sister, then at university, continued to read to me. Once I could read to myself with facility, my most cherished book was, without question, *Whitaker's Almanac* (I would even insist that my mother pack it in our summer holiday trunk).

We were a happy, close-knit family, drawn even closer by my father's premature death. I had two elder sisters, the elder nine years older and the younger five years older than I, so I mostly played alone. We children enjoyed a total emotional security. The atmosphere of our home was certainly religious, but it was neither guilt-ridden nor sanctimonious. (My father was a non-conformist minister.) Its most cherished values were personal responsibility, conscientiousness and gentleness. Uncharitableness, censoriousness and intolerance were held in very low regard. Fear, whether of God or of grown ups, played little part in our upbringing; we were reasoned with, rather than just 'told' how to behave. We were encouraged to be self-reliant, and progressively (perhaps prematurely) taken into our parents' confidence about major decisions.

I look back on my childhood at home as a very happy one; boarding school, though probably 'good' for me, was a traumatic experience which just had to be endured.

I had no chronically unsatisfactory personal relationships for which a private world might have been a compensation.

But the exhilarating sense of power which my 'paracosmic' imagining brought me wasn't *absolute* power. It was subject to the constraints imposed by the imperative demands of realism. I do not think I ever questioned this. I took it for granted that all the fun would go out of this imagining if it were not plausible. Not that a sense of power was anywhere near the *chief* satisfaction which my 'paracosm' provided; a much deeper sense of satisfaction came from the feeling that I was creating order out of chaos, that I really was 'making something' which hadn't existed before.

Silvey's honest account of his own fascination prompts a hard question. What made him, after a successful career at the BBC, return to it late in life when he could 'study' it rather than dabble in it?

DAN AND PETER – 'POSSUMBUL' WORLDS

Dan and Peter were cousins and bosom companions. The mythical state of Possumbul was originally created when they were about 5 years old. Dan thinks that its name may have been a corruption of the 'Possible worlds' much nicer than this one to which the two boys would often hear their socialist fathers refer. Dan was slightly older and was the principal creator, his cousin Peter acting as friendly critic and participator. Possumbul evolved as the boys developed. When they heard of 'languages' (as a subject at school) they invented Possumbulese. Dan's interest in it reached its zenith when he was 10–13, by which time it had become a contemporary island-state, though not impinging on the real world.

Possumbul was a constitutional monarchy and, on the precedent of William-and-Mary, the two boys shared the throne. It shows how young their fantasy started that the heir to the throne was Dan's teddy bear. By 1935 Dan made his heir Edward I, helped perhaps by the fact that Teddy was battered and had lost an eye. There were no children in this world, but they were monarchs, not gods. They could perform no miracles: plausibility was all. Dan recalls a well-meaning adult moving some toy to what he thought a 'better' place without appreciating that such a change in location could not be effected by a hand stretched out from heaven. Moving a toy would call for a crane, a lorry, and some personnel. Similarly the boys were embarrassed by the gift of a mounted toy soldier painted a uniform gold – until they hit upon the expedient of erecting it as a city statue! Realism was all.

At first the boys used their toy soldiers as their citizens, for this was pre-1914, before toy civilians were manufactured.

> But in any case we didn't go in for wars much. . . . Visiting adults used to assume that we made war on each other with our armies, but that would have been out of the question. If we had had a war, one of us would have had to lose. We did, however, invent a sort of Blefuscu for our Lilliput, and called it Possumbile. . . . We made war on Possumbile with a will. . . . I well remember my Quaker mother once reminding me that even enemy soldiers were somebody's sons, and thinking 'Doesn't she realize it's only pretend?'

There was no conscious model for Possumbul, but its character was influenced by, for example, Dan's father's description of India and the many adult discussions of public affairs which the boys overheard. Its history, though realistic, was more interesting and more reassuring than real history. Possumbul had 'no blots on its escutcheon such as those we heard about, like rotten boroughs, public executions, corn laws or colonies'. Possumbul never lost any battles, though, let alone wars. All the same there was an opposition, Tory of course, which was 'hell bent on plunging us all in ruin by a mysterious and sinister intrigue called tariff reform'.

Possumbul was a democracy, but the elections were always won by the Socialists with a thumping majority over the Tory Opposition. Yet the elected government never actually introduced socialism. 'We knew too much about politics even at that early age to expect a victorious party coming into power to carry out its proposals in that crude sort of way.'

The prime minister was a Mr Anderson, a name which may well have been chosen for its similarity to that of Arthur Henderson, the British Labour leader of the time, much admired by the boys' parents. Anderson was perfect, which Henderson, they knew, wasn't. Dan is wryly proud of being a pioneer in rigging elections.

The language, Possumbulese, was too much like English so it was forbidden to write it. Later, they gave it a beautiful script based on Tamil, a primer of which Dan's father had brought back from India.

The boys invented a religion. There was an evil God, Macky-Dougal. The name is telling, Dan thinks. It comes from the bakers *McDougalls*. Their fathers may have told them the bakers were 'up to some nefarious capitalist intrigue'. Dan suffered a bad fall once and blamed it on Macky-Dougal, which led to a ritual. An appeasement ritual was invented – a deliberate and theatrical falling over a hassock, carefully placed for this purpose, would keep Macky-Dougal happy. There was also a Good God who, puritanically, was not to be invoked glibly. A small Victorian phrenological bust became the Good God's image. They built a temple for the Good God out of bricks and play-blocks. Inside, they rigged a torch bulb so it glowed when they turned the playroom light off. It looked very impressive.

The boys used their bricks to build fine cities, peopled by their citizens. Long after he had left toy bricks behind, Dan would spend hours drawing elaborate maps of his capital, Padington (*sic*). There were immigrants, too, a Camel Corps with beautiful tarbushes but much given to demanding tips. All its streets, wide and narrow, would be shown, with its river and docks in blue, its parks in green, and its railways in the colours of their respective liveries. Planning itineraries for Mr Anderson's speaking tours in the suburbs could be an arduous business. As a good socialist, he had no limousine and had to use the regular bus and tram routes and stick to the normal timetables.

Commenting on his description, Dan believes the evolution of their world reflected a growing sense of law. 'We had come to the point of realizing that children, even in their dream world, are bound by rules. . . . A world without rules would, apart from anything else, not be any fun.' Dan found a title for his Utopia, *Noer from Newshere*. (William Morris wrote a book, *News from Nowhere*, which he seems to have adapted.) He felt ambivalent when his father suggested he submit the plan of Padington for a school exhibition of hobbies. In the end, he did. The master in charge said it looked like 'London seen in a delirium' and complained that it was all a terrible waste of map-drawing talent. And why call it Padington? And spell it *wrongly* with one 'd'? Didn't young Dan realize that Paddington was a station, not a town? Crestfallen Dan was asked, 'as I was so hot on maps', to draw one of the Nile – accurate, please, but pretty colours allowed. So much for stimulating the imagination!

Though some of the people in their private world were rounded characters the boys were fascinated less by any personal dramas than by the act of creation, or so they remember, or like to remember. However, 'once created, the elements could not just be demolished and a fresh start made: they had to be amended just as in the real world'. Their world gave expression to their varying interests, in the army, the navy, ships, medals, and even politics. Designing medals, uniforms, and maps gave them an aesthetic delight. 'The fantasy completely saved me from boredom. . . . I was never bored, except when other children wanted to play with me.' It absorbed all his personality over many hours at a time, 'going on into the night, in bed. I was ravished by my world, especially by its beauty and its order.'

Judged by the standards of the time, Dan's upbringing was 'advanced'. He could, and did, talk freely to his parents about anything – including sex. He never felt that his parents failed to take him into their confidence. 'I was seldom punished, and seldom even cussed at.' He had no feelings of being unpredictably 'controlled' or of needing to compensate for problems at home. His parents knew of the fantasy and were mildly encouraging.

The house was full of worthy books. Darwin, Huxley, Marx, and Morris were there, together with tomes on homoeopathy, health, and comparative religion. There were encyclopaedic dictionaries, reference books, and Green's *History of the English People*. The family took the *Daily News* and the *Daily Herald*. Music meant a great deal, but the visual arts less.

Dan was not an early reader: 'perhaps I was read-to too much'. As a little boy he loved myths and legends. His developing tastes in reading followed a familiar pattern: Aesop and Uncle Remus, followed by 'Annuals' and later by Henty, Ballantyne, Jules Verne, and Talbot Baines Reed; 'but I hated books like *A Peep Behind the Scenes, Uncle Tom's Cabin* and *Eric or Little by Little*'. With the coming of adolescence, Dan's character underwent a change so complete that, in retrospect, he regards it as astonishing. He became extroverted, good at games, a gang-leader, and something of a trouble-maker. As he put away childish things, Possumbul became an 'embarrassing memory', not to be recalled until he himself became a father.

Peter also, and quite independently, answered our questionnaire. Though his memories are less vivid than Dan's, they are much the same. He recalls Dan as the leader and intense about the fantasy.

Both of them look back on the 6–12 period as a golden age to which their private world contributed delight.

ADAM – ONE-TRACK MIND?

Adam was a passionate railway enthusiast. At 8 he created an imaginary island, primarily as a scenario for a railway system. Its heyday came when he was 13–14; from 15 onwards he 'found real-life activities more pressing and meaningful'. His interest in places was second only to his interest in railways, so the island grew over the years to accommodate geographical features similar to those – like the Pevensey marshes – which he came to know. To the disgust of his republican friends, the island was a limited monarchy. It was set in modern times but 'it was blissfully secure from events in the real world e.g. it was neutral in wartime, like Sweden'.

An example of a child's fantasy railway world

Although Adam's main preoccupation was with his railway system, when he drew the island's maps and gave its towns and villages Saxon,

French, or Celtic names, he visualized the inhabitants. In drawing up his railway timetables he tried to consider their needs. At one point he devised a language, based on Latin. Later he wrote a series of historical booklets about his railway system.

In organizing this system, he had to observe the normal constraints on railway operation,

> though I indulged fully my love of the devious and obscure. Even the main lines were mostly single-track; I had to arrange crossing-places and connections at junctions, and see that each locomotive got home to the same shed as it had left in the morning. My aim was to provide at least two services a day on any journey.

(This railway was on much better ground technically than Denis's globe-crossing network!)

Adam's railway was a spontaneous creation. For a time, his younger brother imitated him; but this did not last long. Though he mainly played his railway alone, it was not secret. Adam had occasional adult encouragement, but 'my parents so disliked my interest in railway timetables that I was driven to do them furtively'.

Adam was 'supposed to have an IQ of 150 at one stage', but he was frustrated by the limitations of his environment, for he was an inquisitive child and longed to see mountains and castles. He chafed at not being allowed to ride a bicycle until he was 10 because his parents feared he would hurt himself.

Though he learned to read early, he really didn't take to reading until he was an adult, since 'people round me were so obviously wanting me to read more'. He disliked myths and legends, and positively hated Mowgli: 'I sensed instantly that Kipling would dislike me.' His rare visits to the cinema enthralled him: 'I identified strongly with boys in films or plays, but this wasn't anything to do with my island which was a . . . system.'

The family got on all right most of the time though his father 'only came home at week-ends'. Adam's mother was warmer but difficult: 'she seemed to expect too much of me'. There were cultural expectations, too. 'We took *The Times* and that fount of sanity, *The Countryman*. And many heavy books.'

Adam recalls a precise moment when he was 11 when he suddenly became aware of seeing the world 'as an onlooker'. He experienced fantasies of aggression in childhood, for he felt unwanted. He particularly hated his parents 'holding things against me that I could not help, like bed-wetting and being miserable when other children were happy. . . . I longed to be like other boys.' From the age of 6 he felt isolated and unable to discuss his problems with his parents; he 'always dreaded a show-down'. However, Adam does not see that his worlds helped him to cope with his unsatisfactory personal relationships, though it did offer escape and

> a freedom to think and act irrespective of the approval of others. . . . The island was impersonal and totally uncontroversial. It was interesting to me, but not as a source of emotion or conflict. . . . It gave me a satisfying self-respect, and a feeling of achievement which was otherwise lacking at that age.

A slightly more extreme version of railway fantasy was given by George. It seems pointless to reproduce George's world in detail since so much of it was given over to technical details. What is striking is that he concentrated on the transport and garden city arrangements of this world. There were no people and George recalls he was obsessive about order. People were a nuisance.

NORMAN – MORE ONE-TRACK MINDS?

It may be a reflection of the times that many of these accounts were imaginary worlds based on railways.

Norman was 8 or 9 when he created his imaginary island; his interest in it was greatest when he was about 15. By the time he was 18 'it was becoming a tyrant'; three years later it was 'virtually dead'.

The island was originally brought into being to accommodate a fairly extensive Electric Model Railway system. His brother, two years older than Norman, shared in it, but dropped out when he was about 14.

Norman was always fascinated by figures, and first he devised a scale relating time and distance on his island with time and distance in the real world. With Bradshaw as their model, the boys worked out a fairly complicated timetable for their railway system. The island was contemporary, though it had no precise location. Norman was interested in its geography and prepared a map of it. Its place-names were largely inspired by the 'Greyfriars' stories and other comics. Its characters included some famous footballers with whom Norman identified himself. At the time of the Jubilee of the coronation of

King George V and Queen Mary, the island sent a deputation to London. Norman's main interest, however, was in the creation of his 'paracosm', not in the dramas of its characters. The one exception was football. Later, Norman, who was a soccer fan, worked out 'a very sophisticated football league system, arranging matches by identifying island teams with the English Football League fixtures, as given in the *Athletic News* football annuals'. He published monthly league tables in an island magazine, *The Reporter*, for about eight years.

> The matches themselves were played by my adapting a real game in which a goal was scored each time one of the steel balls was lifted on one of the wooden spades, and popped into a container. As soon as one missed, that was the end of the game. The trouble was that I became the world's expert at this game, and then had to make deliberate misses, so mentally favouring the teams to which I was particularly partial!

It was a secret world. Only his elder brother, who was his close friend, knew of its existence. Until he read Robert Silvey's appeal in the Press, Norman had never heard of any other children having private worlds. He now thinks that his did encourage him to ferret out facts about the real world, and help him towards a better understanding of it. Music was an example of that. He devised a radio service for his island. Though he liked only pop music, he saw the need to cater for all tastes. Grappling with the problems of programme planning made him listen to jazz and classical music, which he came to like.

Norman believes that the fantasy helped him to deal with real problems. His mother had died when he was 3 and, when his father remarried, he felt that his stepmother devoted more attention to the children of that marriage than to his brother or himself. As a result, once his brother went to boarding school, Norman felt very much alone at home. The island gave him 'immense satisfaction from having an absorbing interest which no other person could change or destroy, and which in all respects was *my* world, free from outside influences unless I allowed it'. The failure of his parents to know him became clear. 'Curiously, my parents often expressed the view that I could show more imagination. Perhaps this was true in relation to their world; but I was very imaginative in relation to mine.' He could read at 5, and remembers loving *Gulliver's Travels* and religious books. Though theirs was not a particularly religious home, Norman was encouraged to go to Sunday School and to be a chorister.

ALLAN – ADULTS' IDEA?

Allan is the only person who believes his private world was suggested by an adult. It 'derived from the map of an island drawn for me by my father and containing such imaginative concepts as a Land of Lost Toys and a Land of Upside Down People'. Allan was then about 9. Serviceable though these reach-me-down imaginings were at first, he soon outgrew them and developed 'something far more prosaic – a sort of ideal welfare state (called Weltonia)'. This had, yet again, a highly developed public transport system. Public transport was, throughout his childhood, his paramount, though not his only, interest. Interestingly he felt that he was not very good at mechanical things. Allan was about 13 when Weltonia most fascinated him.

For his nearest sibling, a younger sister, he created another country, Celtamania, of which she was monarch. Other countries followed, including Kish-Koshum, which was an aggressive power and ruled by a mad dictator. A number of the 1930s imaginary worlds had, not surprisingly, mad dictators. Did they know, given their passion for public transport, that Mussolini made the trains run on time? This imaginary universe served more than one purpose. On the one hand, it served as the location for imaginary games with Allan's sister and his friends – games of the cops-and-robbers variety; on the other hand it was also 'a sort of workshop for ideas on the subjects which, from time to time, were of interest to me'. This universe had its own cosmology. 'God had decided in the mists of prehistory to have a contest. He created exactly the same conditions on two widely separated planets and then, as it were, sat back to await results.' Eventually Weltonia turned out to be 'the superior world, where poverty had been abolished and peace was maintained by an international police force'.

Despite its unlikely creation with God as spectator, Allan felt it vital that Weltonia was plausible. 'Although Weltonia was too much like the real world to allow much scope for imagination, it was at least something I had created.' The system rather than any characters dominated the fantasy. Three-dimensional people were not important.

There was nothing particularly secret about Allan's private world. When he went to boarding school, he wrote, for his little sister's benefit, a textbook on Weltonia which he showed to some of his school-friends, so starting something of a craze for private worlds.

He was the middle child of a family of seven; four girls and two other boys. His father was frequently away from home; and when he was there, there was frequent quarrelling between the parents which Allan hated to hear. When Allan was 14, his father died in the London Blitz and thereafter the family circumstances were strained, but they continued to consider themselves as 'among the cultural elite of their town'.

GODFREY – GOODBYE TO ALL THAT FANTASY

Godfrey is now an artist. He cannot recall whether he indulged in any world-weaving before, at the age of 10, he created Dobid. Dobid was an island state to which Godfrey subsequently added three neighbouring colonial islands. These four islands fascinated him until he was 15, when he deliberately set them aside to concentrate on working for his matriculation. That examination behind him, he turned back to his private world; but a year later (and not before he had written a moving valediction) he ceased altogether to work on it. The demands of reality had become too great. By this time he was 17.

Dobid's location was never clearly defined. Nor was its place in time; but it had its contemporary features. There were tramcars, acetylene-powered aircraft and some impressive engineering achievements, such as sea-bridges. It was a monarchy and had a peerage. Godfrey envisaged some of its exalted personages, but says he did not identify with any of them.

Dobid had 'enormous problems, though things were never allowed to get out of hand'. The neighbouring islands caused many problems. Their people, culture, and language were relatively primitive. Constitutionally Dobid could not acquire new territory by conquest; it had to be bought. There was an ancient Dobidian language. It was now no longer spoken; but Godfrey wrote on vellum a number of historic documents in its script. At the age of 12 he was already exhibiting his literary and artistic aptitudes, writing his first book, a *History of Dobid*, and designing elaborate maps and heraldry.

Godfrey 'gradually embodied' in Dobid the things he was interested in. Its ability to evolve sustained it over all those years, but at all times everything about it had to be plausible. The fantasy was solitary but not secret: his parents knew about it. This was a mixed blessing as they would sometimes get him to show his documents and maps to visiting adult friends. Often they tittered, which irritated Godfrey so that he tried to avoid such requests.

Godfrey was the youngest of six children, four girls and two boys; they were a reasonably harmonious family. Godfrey was closest to his brother. He recalls that whenever they met children they had not met before (as at a party) they would afterwards decide which ones they had 'got'. This meant those whom they thought that, theoretically, they could dominate or succour in an imaginary emergency. It wasn't directly related to Dobid but parallel.

Godfrey's world engaged his interest from 10 to 17 years of age. Even at 17 it was very unwillingly that Godfrey decided to give it up. He took formal leave of his world and wrote a valedictory, of which what follows is an extract:

The end, 25th July, 1928

It is too much. I find I can continue this hobby no longer. I find these friends of mine are leading me into madness. They have been my dearest friends for seven years now and I find I can go no farther with Them. To step one step farther is to start on a long, long trail thinking out, writing and drawing a nation in full detail.

The growing size of the books I have chosen is but typical of the hobby. It has gradually grown until, at the moment, it is on the verge of absurdity. Thus have gone all my hobbies, my dearest hobbies of which I may perhaps tell later, but they were never dearer than this. They have grown from a game to a craze, a craze to a hobby, and from a hobby to become party (*sic*) of my very self.

Now at the age of seventeen I am about to start my real life. My intention is to be an artist; a life of continual study to which I look forward, will consequently demand all my time. I have much to say – Doubt if I shall remember it all – I find daily that my interest in life about me grows considerably and I feel that I should spend no time on the Dobidians.

They have been the happiest part of my life. The Dobidians were more than a hobby to me and I thank God for them. They have been a means of uniting my every craze and hobby into one great nation of friends. My feeling towards the Dobidians are indescribable. . . .

I find that though to practice my hand in various branches of art, to work out my Dobidian ambitions, would be a good means, yet I find that when I am called upon to show my best samples of work, I have only Dobidian things to show and these invite the interest of many strangers into the Dobidians, wherefore I feel embarrassed and foolish, not caring to explain them fully for the lengthiness of their history. Accordingly I have determined to sever any connection with these men and devote myself to my studies and to the things of the world around me.

No one else seems to have written such a formal farewell.

ROSALIND – MAKING UP FOR MOTHER?

When Rosalind was 4 or 5, she invented two imaginary companions, Jean and Robert. 'I objected to adults sitting in a certain chair when Robert was already occupying it.' She endowed her toys, both dolls and animals, with human characteristics and thought of them as her own and Robert's children. When she was about 10, she and her 8-year-old sister each created an imaginary island. Four years later the islands were superseded by an imaginary girls' boarding school. This was 'the peak of invention'.

The islands were contemporary and situated close to the British Isles. 'Jean and Robert came to live there; but an earlier friend of ours, Dr Craven A, had been abandoned by then.' Rosalind, being the elder, was the initiator and leader. Her island was Santafagasta and its principal city was Quong. Despite the exotic names, English was spoken. Rosalind was more interested in her island's geography than its history, and recalls drawing its map.

For her, 'creation and further creation was more important than imaginary happenings and acting them out'. In this process of creation, she felt an obligation to be plausible, 'which was quite restrictive' upon the free play of her imagination. Her private world brought her 'a sense of power, control and importance which gave security. . . . I enjoyed its orderliness, yet there was excitement too.' Their islands had no specific model, but they were inspired by Stevenson's *The Land of Counterpane*. While their imaginary islands were not secret, no other children participated in them. (Rosalind notes that later on her own children showed no inclination to be paracosmists.)

When the girls were 8 and 6 respectively, their mother died suddenly, and they were placed in the care of an aunt whom previously they had hardly known. Two years later their father remarried but their relationship to their stepmother was not a wholly happy one. She tended to treat them as younger than they were, and the girls resented this. But Rosalind says that her childhood was 'happy on the whole'.

Rosalind thinks her fantasy helped her to cope with the loss of her mother, to whom she was devoted, and with her subsequent problems. Her father, who was a doctor and by nature a 'merry' man, became remote and withdrawn after his first wife died, and never spoke to the children about their mother.

Rosalind was, she says, a bright, curious, and conscientious little girl who got on well with other children. An early reader, she loved myths and legends, 'though they sometimes frightened me'. Until she was 7, she lived in a town and her greatest delight was being taken into the country. Her 'hate' was 'bullying small boys'. In all, there were three sisters but she was really close only to the second.

It was a non-conformist home, and her parents were well read, well educated, and interested in the arts and in travel. Discipline was based on reasoning, though her father could be stern. He was also tolerant and gentle. Her mother was more erratic; sometimes gay, sometimes depressed. Rosalind enjoyed her school life, both at a progressive co-ed day school till 11 and afterwards at boarding school. Her 'paracosm' does seem to have been produced at a time of acute stress when she had lost her mother and had to settle to a new, far from perfect, step-mother. But she didn't, therefore, create a world of domestic bliss. The fantasy was indirect. To suggest that children make up worlds where everything is all right, conflicts are ironed out in play, is too crude. The very act of imagining and acting out may in itself be relief. And fun.

LEONARD – SMALL BALTIC NATION SURVIVES

It was not until Leonard started at secondary school that he began to think of creating a dream world. At first 'these were just Ruritanian ideas buzzing around in my head', but within three years he had created in his imagination a highly developed contemporary state. During the summer holidays of his fifteenth year he produced in manuscript a volume running to more than 20,000 words, the title page of which is inscribed: 'Luftstaad, an account of an imaginary Baltic state from its first years to the present, as well as the story of its social and political cultures'. Below the title is a line of text in Xaalic, the language he devised, with its own script; and the volume includes three historical maps. Soon after he completed this considerable task, Leonard's interest declined.

Luftstaad (which means 'free-country') occupied the island of Gatska Sandon, midway between Sweden and Estonia. It was a republic, with a population of nearly a quarter of a million. Its capital was the city of Luftstaaden. Iron and zinc were mined on the island. Oats, wheat, and flax were cultivated, and it was famous for its 'herds of superbly fine cattle', which earned 'high profits from the Scandinavian markets for their high-class breeding qualities'. There was also a flourishing fishing industry. Its people were of 'Indo-European stock; Protestant religion'.

Leonard's history reveals that Gatska Sandon was colonized at the end of the eighteenth century by Estonian refugees fleeing Russian oppression. In 1800 they elected their first king, Iskor I. Over the next 150 years, Luftstaad had an eventful and continually changing history. Periods of economic and social progress were interrupted by various wars. The country was occupied by the Swedes, the Russians, the Germans, and the Russians again. All this turmoil was set out in Leonard's long record, with dramatic details of the wars and crises, and vivid vignettes of the country's successive kings and its one vicious dictator.

In 1954 a new welfare system was introduced which included universal retirement pensions at 60. A fine ideal but 'such was the amount of work to be done and the character and toughness of the Staadians, that many workers did not retire until 68'. Also, the closeness of the Soviet Union forced Luftstaad to arm itself with the latest rocketry. It boasted it would resist any aggression. It also suppressed its native Communist Party.

Leonard was uncritical of the Staadians. He rhapsodized: 'no one must think that Luftstaad has so nationalistic a character that she would be opposed to any Union of Mankind. Indeed no higher aspiration lingers in any Staadian mind than that of a World Federation.' But this pious sentiment is followed by a somewhat chilling note: 'Luftstaad has great need to expand herself as a young nation. . . . It is a pity that there are no, or very few, lands to which she can lay claim.' Luftstaad may be imaginary but it sounds very familiar.

All these details were summarized from the long and great work on the history of the Baltic states. It is hardly surprising to learn that Leonard was 'fascinated by history, especially military history and naval warfare'; he was also interested in politics.

The inspiration to write came from books, mostly military. . . . I was fascinated by the histories of small democratic states, especially the Baltic states of Finland, Estonia, Latvia and Lithuania. Much stimulus came from a second-hand copy of J. Hampden Jackson's *Estonia*. . . . The characters in the history of Luftstaad were essentially historical figures and I do not recall identifying with any of them. . . . There was an obligation to be plausible, and how frustrating I found it!

Leonard did not share his world with any contemporary until a fairly late stage when he 'did share the idea with a class-mate . . . but I did not really like his more practical outlook and the co-operation soon ceased'. His parents knew nothing of it. When he was surrounded by reference books, gazetteers, and atlases and he worked on it, they thought he was doing his homework. Leonard is sure that it helped him with his school-work.

It was for him a way of escaping from what he felt to be a 'deadly dull' world, and was also, perhaps, a substitute for personal relationships, for he was a 'loner'. Research was a joy and it made him feel self-sufficient.

Leonard was an early reader, avidly devouring comics and later Enid Blyton and W.E. Johns, and also history and 'factual' books, particularly – hardly surprising – books about the Baltic states of Scandinavia.

An important personal influence was his maternal grandmother, who had married a sea captain. 'She told me stories of my grandfather and his travels. She encouraged me to read his many books and bought many for me. I cannot (over-) estimate her influence on my imaginative development!' She died just before he wrote the history.

Leonard was an only child. The family got on well together, though Leonard thought his father, a crane-driver, very strict. All the books in their house were Leonard's. The family paper was the *Daily Mirror*; no interest was taken in any of the arts. 'My father detested my interest in classical music on the radio.'

He does not recall having fantasies of aggression or any conscious awareness of an ability to view himself with detachment. Until he was 14, Leonard was a 'tall weakling. . . . There was a fair bit of bullying in the lower streams of a predominantly working-class bilateral [school]. . . . Most of my friends were fairly introverted too.' His greatest joy as a child was 'being successful and gaining the admiration of my peers'. He also derived deep satisfaction from mastering a subject (like the Navy), and feeling an 'expert' on it. What he most hated was being shown up in front of his peers. But he looks back on his childhood as 'generally happy, except between 11 and 13, when school was a traumatic experience'.

AMBROSE – OPERATIC

Ambrose comes from a distinguished New England academic family, in which imaginary worlds are a tradition. When he was introduced to the idea by his father, a geographer, it appealed to him at once. His sister did not take to it nor did Ambrose's own children when, in due course, he told them about it. Ambrose was always conscious of his family's tradition. They were clever, literary, and distinguished. Tempers were always kept under control; arguments were rational. His father introduced him to many artistic pursuits.

'I was about 12 when I drew the map which fixed my own country in its definite shape, though I had parts of it – the names and the maps of some of the cities – already.' This was shortly after the family had made a five-month trip to Europe. His father gave Ambrose a big bound book of blank pages to use as he pleased, which stimulated the fantasy. 'My interest in my country as such was probably at the peak for the next two years.' After that, Ambrose tended to use it simply to express specific interests as his imaginary baseball league. 'It was pretty well dead by the time I was 17.'

From first till last it was a continent, about the size of Australia. There did not seem to be room for it anywhere on Earth, so he located it on an 'earth-sized moon of Saturn'. This, however, caused complications. 'I had to invent all sorts of reasons for how the people got there; why the language developed as it did, and why so many particulars resembled things on Earth.'

It was a contemporary society. 'Many phenomena of the real world were closely imitated in my world. These tended to be places and things (my world had a city like Venice, for example) . . . rather than events.' Ambrose wrote an historical account of his country, 'but, generally speaking, individual characters did not play a significant role', though some had specific functions.

At first, Ambrose was king of his world, but this too raised problems of plausibility and protocol for 'the members of my family were the Royal Family, and it took quite a bit of monkey business to explain why it was that both my uncle and his sons, and my father, renounced their claims to the throne in my favour'. Ambrose was interested in ships, railroads, baseball, and opera, and it showed.

I drew maps. I composed charts and the tables. I made up railroad timetables, composed locomotive rosters, assigned locomotives to trains. Composed an opera season. Invented an imaginary baseball game, by means of which I was able to create a baseball season. In general my interest seems to have been in establishing regularities; though sometimes I would indulge in a fantasy, projecting myself into the timetable.

The most important thing which Ambrose now feels he learned from his 'paracosmic' experience was about 'how the imagination works. . . . It helped me to become vividly aware of the power and limits of fantasy.' The pleasures seem simple in retrospect.

It was an attempt to get some kind of control over the real world by reproducing its appearances; to find order in it, and to put myself in relation to that. Personal ego satisfaction was *not*, as I remember, usually very important, though it may have been occasionally. The deeper motive and satisfaction, however, was in the attempt to look closely at some part of the world by making an imitation of it. . . . I think it is an essentially artistic motivation, not unrelated to the composing of novels by the adult novelist.

As a novelist, as well as an academic, Ambrose writes: 'I think there is a connection between the kind of discomfort that caused me to create an imaginary country as a child, and what causes me to write novels to-day.' Like Miriam, he sees a link which may be true for him, but one wonders why so few of MacKeith and Silvey's original sample of fifty-seven became artists.

JACK – STILL AN ISLAND?

Jack wrote: 'From my very earliest days the market garden my father owned beside our home was a town to me, where I drove the trams and trolley buses. Each part of the town had its own name.' Jack and a school-friend who developed his own town would often lay each town out in the living-room. The tram and trolley bus system was 'the main interest. My interest in trams and trolley buses remains; I am now 38.' And this love of trams affected Jack's imagination:

From early teenage years I created an imaginary island in the North Sea. . . . This was an *imaginary* island, but *not fantastic*. It was supposed to be in all respects *realistic*, with roads, railways, towns, hills and other geographical features.

At first it was called Saxonland, but I soon changed the name to Cwayland. From the start the people of the island spoke their own language, with hardly any words like English.

At one stage I wrote a Cwaylan history, but it was difficult to dovetail it into real-life events. Easier was mythology; it was fun inventing an old religion, like the Greek or Norse. The development of the language was the principal enjoyment I got out of the island. I tried several experiments – dialects of English, a language with an entirely alien vocabulary, French, and finally a 'realistic' language formed of a mix of previous ideas, Anglo-Saxon, Old Norse and other odd words. It slowly developed in grammar, vocabulary, and literature.

Most of what Jack wrote in Cwaylan consisted of weather forecasts and news bulletins. Imitating the Eisteddfod, Cwayland had its annual cultural festival, the Londiunandid, with appropriately colourful ceremonies.

Jack hung on to most of the literature he produced, though 'my Cwaylan is a bit rusty now'; he did provide an example:

Ner steniten pui Ofllerd (lusty foulen elt: Tarnoc) an li twelstu Mornedd. Ii mustu, u nwyn-bu au wif, waian, y anet wairn, au y Termac. Eu, Ofllerd, mustu y smelld, o y felc lerte, Tu, twelustu lifarnedd an fein men recc t'un ust Ofllerd.

This was suitably epic: it meant

'Never started' or 'Without beginning' was Ofllerd (known in old Cwaylan as Tarnoc) and he dwelt in Morn. He made himself a *wif* or wife, Waron, the first woman and the Chief Goddess. The Ofllerd made the Smelld or Lordly People. They lived in Ilfard, a plain made for them by Ofllerd.

Jack reckoned that the style of the Genesis of Cwaylan was suitably old-fashioned. 'Every time I drew a map of Cwayland, it changed its shape as I searched for satisfaction. I've kept all the maps and almost everything I ever wrote or drew about the island.' Jack also devised lists of local radio and television programmes because the island had its own television station. His father once found a page of this and scribbled 'rubbish' over it.

He worried about accuracy. 'I was intensely interested in my island's geography, and always found it frustrating that I had no real knowledge of geology and could never be sure whether my geological features were realistic.' Jack was always careful not to violate the yet-to-be-created *Guinness Book of Records*. 'There were no extra long railway tunnels or extra high mountains' but he did allow himself frequent and very dramatic storms. In general, 'things were normal'. Imaginary individuals did not play much part in Jack's private world.

> I don't think I lived on the island myself . . . but I did 'visit' it and I was a Doctor of Cwayland. . . . I vaguely remember conferring an honorary degree on my friend, so it is probable that I took various roles as the fancy took me.

He had a colour scheme of different coloured gowns for different kinds of degrees.

> I certainly made Cwayland fit into the everyday run of affairs. I once drew a map showing constituencies, for example. Conservatives held most seats, followed by Labour in more industrial areas, and one Liberal seat in the North-West. Cwayland had its own ITV company, Teledaw Fon, and the usual BBC networks; and I often wrote out lists of programmes. I also planned transmitters and channels, and had constant problems with the somewhat mountainous terrain.

Except for his personal friend, no one, not even his parents, knew about Jack's 'paracosm'. His friend imitated him, creating Augland, later Norland, in the North Sea. This, too, had a complex trolley bus system.

> My parents would see me drawing maps, but did not ask me anything about it; but I know my father thought it was rubbish. . . . I was never *forbidden* to continue any of my strange hobbies, thank goodness. I never talked to any outsiders about it, as I was afraid of their condemnation and possible teasing, I suppose.
>
> As an adult, I confess to you that I still have an island in the North Sea. It is a descendant of Cwayland and very occasionally I draw a new map of it. . . . You must think I am hardly in touch

with the real world, but I am. . . . I have hardly told anyone about Cwayland; but yours is obviously a sympathetic ear, and it is reassuring to think that my unusual pastime is maybe not so strange after all.

As he was a young teenager when he was most interested in Cwayland, Jack wasn't a great reader. But he was 'tremendously impressed with the Viking myths, and moved quickly into writing myths for Cwayland'. It never occurred to him, he says, to cast himself as the leader in Cwayland. But Cwayland allowed him to play 'at what you can never really get to be – everything from God to local transport manager'.

Jack did not experience childhood as difficult. The world did not help him cope with problems 'in any direct sense' but he loved retreating into it. He also hugged to himself the secret truth that, though he might not seem to be much to others, he could create. 'Look I can create and run a whole island and you think I can do nothing much. And you don't even know.'

PAUL – PHARAOH PHANTASIES

Paul, now a science-fiction writer and an artist, started creating private worlds in early adolescence. 'They were all basically similar, in the sense of being peoples occupying lands. . . . They were mystical/comical; usually linked with a real land (e.g. Egypt) in a fictional guise.' His final world, the empire of Makrimanztec, was created when he was 15. He worked with a school-friend whose special interest was the Gothic novel, 'which I knew nothing about'.

Paul's great interests were geography, history, and archaeology. During boring geometry lessons, when their master spent most of the period with his back toward the class scribbling on the board, the two boys occupied their time in inventing 'silly names' for their characters. Several silly name characters starred in later adventures and Paul believes the Goons freed their imagination though not in relation to their subject matter.

There survives a 'History' of Makrimanztec in an exercise book of fifty-six closely written pages. It contains a list of the rulers from legendary times (pre-8000 BC) to the present day; they total over 1,000, and even though the same names frequently recur, the list includes over 200 invented names. Many of these had nonsense names.

There was the Pharaoh Isocells:Haroo-hatepec:Foro Poo LII and that close relation of Isocells, Paralelalls, who was another geometric king. There was also Telchemetek-Rhalukemen Selchetumenen IV, a monarch who may not have the longest reign but certainly had the longest name. Other Pharaohs range from Raflekht I in the legendary period, Aykrivik in 4590 BC, and IntefX early in the Christian era, to Rex-Georges XII, who came to the throne in 1932 and was reigning at the time the 'History' was written.

There are notes against each reign, some recording the archaeological evidence of cities built or historical events. Many of these notes are facetious. Thus we learn that King Ay I (7 BC) was deaf, and was given his name because to every question he answered 'Eh?' or 'Ay?'; that one of his successors 'was not used to ruling because he had never done it before'; that the mummified hand of Queen Mukhamen was 'eaten by archaeological explorers before they knew what it was', and that King Mu-Uy (4000 BC) 'often looked as though he were alive'. But how?

A volcanic eruption, known as the Great Upheaval, cut the empire off from the outside world in 2400 BC. It was not rediscovered until 1870, but we learn of its progress in the intervening centuries. About AD 1000 there were great improvements in medicine, an elected Senfet was created to rule the country, and schools for the nobility and gentry were founded. These were extended to the population as a whole, 'except madmen', two centuries later. The seventeenth century saw the formation of an Anti-Corruption League. Steam power was discovered in 1800 under King Moxdos-Rex IX.

With the opening up of Makrimanztec, two archaeological expeditions revealed the story of the ancient empire. The first was led by Sir Sirrah Ponsonby-Jarf, and the second by Sir Joseph Swivelbody. The English explorers behaved in the best tradition of the Raj and the Goons. Sir Sirrah befriended and conned the King Rex Makimlek IX, giving him a set of red beads and a mirror. Sir Sirrah was followed by a series of 'pith-helmetted idiot heroes' including the British equivalent of Isocelles, Sir Seven Equation Brown. There was also Sir Hitler Substance-Flank and his cook Stanislew Cyczwskhev-Czski of Zclezcvvikia. (What did his recipes sound like?) Paul's favourite idiot was Sir Sirrah who probably looted the national flag, a paint rag. His friend's favourite was Sir Kunzle Butter. Sadly, Paul noted: 'My collaborator died while the rest of us were sitting School Certificate. It was a short illness. Perhaps he lives in the Great Gondel in the Sky.'

The entire work runs to well over 10,000 words. It includes several carefully drawn maps, together with illustrations of the national flag and of the Rhusttan stone which made possible a deciphering of the ancient language, Grukh.

Paul says that the two boys 'explored the limits, as we saw them, of imaginative licence', and that he never lost interest in his imaginary empire. Rather it grew into an interest in science fiction. At the time, he says, 'it cushioned me from the terrible world of snobbish housing estate adolescence of the 1940s'. He was a very early reader, and 'self-aware' at a very young age. When he was 12, he saw people dancing in the streets on VE-Day. He recalls thinking 'how shallow adults were; don't they realize that wars don't end as easily as that?' In adolescence, he experienced 'sometimes suicidal' self-doubt. His greatest joys were in reading and being alone; though his mother would chide him for not being outside, enjoying himself, instead of 'stuck in the house with my nose in a book'.

He had one brother, younger than himself. Although the family was superficially close-knit, he never really got on with his parents or his brother. His parents were, he says, 'staggeringly dull'. The values in his home were conventional, but 'I never really knew *why* we did anything'. He describes his childhood as 'mixed. Very insecure'.

At school he particularly resented the way in which subjects would be taught without any attempt to show how they related to the real world. As to his relationships with his peers, he knew himself to be 'odd'. He was too tall to be bullied, but 'at the time I couldn't imagine being missed if I dropped dead'. Paul's style, like his worlds, had an unusual degree of wit. And his 'paracosm' had a practical outlet in his science-fiction.

JEREMY

Jeremy was always fascinated by languages. At 13 he invented Ktu, and then created the Republic of Ktu so that there should be a country in which it was spoken. The state was located on another planet, to which Jeremy had been 'transported accidentally'. He thinks he was influenced by Ruritania and Novello's invention of Krasnia in *Glamorous Night*.

Jeremy's memory of the structure and institutions of Ktu is now rather vague, but he recalls that it had a national anthem and a currency. Personalities and their rivalries had no part in this imagining. It was solely as a vehicle for its language, which was highly sophisticated. Jeremy 'built it up with its own words until they reached about one hundred, and then constructed rules for forming everything else from English. It also had its own script.' He wrote a Ktu grammar. It was important to him that the language should be logical and plausible. 'Some things worried me': given that Ktu was another planet, why did it resemble English so much? 'But I couldn't help that.' Jeremy still remembers the language and sent Robert Silvey a number of entries of its script, most of it on the pages of a diary with more prosaic events like 'staff meetings' pencilled in. If Silvey were interested and genuine, Jeremy even offered to rewrite the lost grammar. Once banknotes, newspapers, and other material existed in Ktu. Jeremy took Russian: the Cyrillic alphabet fascinated him and he had 'a longing to know what N meant backwards'. The original grammar fitted an 8 x 7 exercise book. Jeremy sent Silvey the Lord's Prayer in Ktu though he never seems to have wondered why, on another planet, they should have the same Lord's Prayer.

No adults knew about Ktu, but it became something of a vogue amongst Jeremy's school-friends, to whom he would show Ktu's banknotes, newspapers, etc., as illustrations of the language in use, and to some of whom he would lend the Ktu grammar. 'I had great satisfaction from the eventual completeness of Ktu and my fluency, both written and oral, in it.' The republic faded away during Jeremy's adolescence; but his loyalty to the language remained – he uses it for his private notes to this day. His wife and children don't know what Ktu really is – the relic of a childish game he finds useful.

At 13 Jeremy was, he thinks, a bright, imaginative, reliable, and self-confident boy. He had had polio as a child, from which he did not fully recover until he was grown up.

He says that, as a boy, he always found it easy to view himself objectively. He was an early reader, but 'particularly disliked anything he was told was a classic'. His childhood at home was very happy, but he disliked school. 'I hated being driven all the time and having everything prescribed down to the letter'; but he persisted with the interest in language. 'I took Russian as a major subsidiary in my degree.' The Cyrillic alphabet continued to fascinate and the pull of exotic languages remained strong.

Chapter Five

UNSTRUCTURED, SHIFTING, AND IDYLLIC WORLDS

There are some worlds which do not seem to fit any of the themes. They are not based mainly on toys or railways; there are no romantic escapades. The three worlds that follow include what seem to be two of the most interesting. Francis's twin worlds suggest that, as a child, he yearned for a kind of tranquillity, which made his choice of career odd: he became a soldier. And Deborah created a world with a frenzied mixture of biblical images because, it seems, that was just what she needed.

FRANCIS - MAKE MINE MITTY

Francis, now retired after a distinguished military career, had two 'paracosms' which overlapped in time. World 1 was 'a Walter Mitty affair in which I had much success for my family', and in which he 'identified with military heroes'. Its events were implausible and largely inspired by books and stories. World 2 was quite different, both in form and in function; he created it spontaneously when he was about 7. The different worlds had different rituals. Francis had to think before entering the Mitty world; entering the second world required no effort.

'It was sometimes an island, sometimes a territory with mountains, roads, etc. - not always inhabited', but he did not like its form to change. He drew maps of it, which his mother lost. Though it had no precise location, it was a precise place, a 'well-defined territory'. He knew when he was in it. He had no conscious model for it though he had travelled much in Egypt and India as a child. These places left him with a keen sense of their atmosphere which permeated his World 2. Though it was contemporary, he didn't incorporate in it any real public or private events. 'In it I saw, touched and felt things. Other beings, human or animal, came and went without any particular effect on me.' He felt that the imagining of World 2 was subject to 'some form of limitation which, if broken, would ruin it'. He cannot define this 'beyond that it was intangible and somewhat strange'. In Mittyland, though, he could strut as a perfect hero.

'No conscious effort by me was necessary to enter this world, as opposed to World 1; it just unfolded as I walked.' In it he 'was very happy, did nothing in particular but just loved being there. It was a happy, enjoyable, un-evil place.' He often was in a street or park and transported into his second, dreamy world. In retrospect, Francis wonders if its serenity had not something Utopian about it though he didn't, when he was 7, know what Utopian meant. He came back to describing his feelings in World 2 as being best caught by Wordsworth's 'trailing clouds of glory from when they come' (*sic*). Francis added that he was religious and respected Hindu ideas. He added the odd rider that, despite this, he did not enter his private world as a result of fasting. He feels that his World 2 satisfied his lifelong deep sense of order and his hatred of destruction (feelings which were his even when, in war, he had to destroy as part of his duty). 'My sons are amused at my inability to enjoy the destruction of old crockery with balls at a fun fair. In my private world all was clean, tidy and undamaged.'

Although World 2 was very much Francis's private domain, he was not a natural 'loner' and prided himself on being good with men. Didn't he command regiments? But the private worlds continued to matter. 'It appeared very important to have my private world almost as if my brain, or my soul, needed it.'

Francis started his world when he was 7. His interest peaked when he was 14 and then palled though, even as an adult soldier, he occasionally fell back to it. One of Francis's greatest pleasures as a small boy was hearing his mother, whom he adored, retell stories of her father's adventures in India at the time of the Mutiny. The boy's relationship with his mother was not such, however, that he could tell her everything. It meant a great deal to him that his mother and family should be happy: 'a family upset or row worried me greatly'. He was generally happy in his childhood, 'taking the rough with the smooth without undue care . . . I look back on my childhood and innocence with nostalgic affection'.

To Freedom, Justice, Beauty, Heroism . . . I remember vaguely

BRENDA

At about the age of 9, Brenda can remember creating two private worlds and there may have been more. Each of these had a similar context – a kind of mystical harmonious society. Brenda's world resounded with ideas of freedom, justice, beauty, and heroism and it was 'more closely associated with feelings than ideas'. As a result, it was rather amorphous: 'there were productive units and social interactions'. She could produce only one specific memory though:

> Each world was definitely a place with very clear strong boundaries. One fantasy was enacted in a copse . . . which no one else seemed to visit. The other was simply a map I drew of an imaginary island, which incorporated similar vague notions of an ideal way of life.

There was no conscious model – Brenda had little idea of history or geography which is why, she thinks, it was mostly emotional.

It was very important indeed to be plausible, in that everything had to connect into a coherent system, or whole pattern. Two-dimensional characters were not important. Creating places where things happened was the major preoccupation; but there was imaginary acting-out of social interactions.

Hazily she thinks she had a number of magic worlds. Less hazily she remembers trying to get other children to take part 'but they didn't seem to understand'. She was frightened they might make fun of her. After about two years these worlds 'gradually became unsatisfactory and depressing, and were all over by the time I went to Grammar School'.

It was important to Brenda that adults should *not* know about it. As with children she feared she would be made fun of. Was Brenda creating a world because of her family? Her father was a farmer. He was a dominating, authoritarian figure who, during most meals, boomed his political opinions much like 'Alf Garnett'. He admired 'muck and brass', and Brenda often hated him because of the way he treated her mother. There was constant conflict between her parents.

It was a 'horsey' family. Brenda and her mother both loved riding: it was a bond. Brenda kept a pony diary; she was constantly nagged to look after her pony. She describes her childhood as 'vaguely unhappy'. Most of the time she was left to her own devices, which encouraged her to wallow in her isolation, perhaps. 'I was called lazy if I was reading a book.' She started to read fairly late, but by 9 was reading widely. She particularly recalls the deep impression made on her by reading *How Green was my Valley*. 'School very nearly destroyed me. It was a terrible endurance test for my emotions. . . . I was dreadfully over-sensitive. . . . I always felt myself to be odd and "different".' Yet, for all that, her fantasy lasted only two years and she was slightly embarrassed by how little she could recall of it. Perhaps definite fantasies leave the strongest memories?

DEBORAH – A SAFE PLACE

Deborah was born in 1939. She was the seventh child of a poor family, and her mother died giving birth to her. Relatives took over four of the children, and the other two, with Deborah, were placed in the local authority's children's home. Soon one of her sisters was adopted and, six years later, so were Deborah and her other sister. However, Deborah felt 'totally bewildered and alien to this new life'. She has many disturbing memories. Within a year she was returned to the children's home, though her sister remained with the same adopting couple. It seems clear that her fantasy world was a reaction to all this insecurity.

A short time later, Deborah went to live with an uncle and aunt who had an 8-year-old son, but had previously lost a daughter in an accident. 'Again I felt alien; as if I were obliged to "belong", yet didn't.' She was constantly badly compared with the lost daughter. 'I was often confused as to my role.' This situation became impossible; she was returned to the children's home, where she remained until she went to the local grammar school at the age of 11.

Deborah was then fostered by a couple in the Salvation Army, where she was extremely unhappy. Once more she was returned to the children's home, and there she stayed until she completed her education at the age of 17. 'Incidentally, the normal school-leaving age was then 14, so again I was a bit of an oddity.'

Deborah found refuge from all these tensions in a private world. She cannot remember when it first started or how. 'It is as if it was always there. Certainly it altered over the years in that now [she is in her 40s] it has become a very complex sphere.' It had no formal structure, geographical or historical, but consisted exclusively of 'people'. 'The people in it were my family. I "saw" them. They were my security, my friends, my guardians. It was my real world. The only place I felt safe.' Many of her 'people' were totally imaginary creations, but some of the most important were based on real people, though she sometimes endowed these with different personalities. She would converse at length with her 'people', often out loud, even though she worried. 'People told me that only mad people talk to themselves.' She was often punished for 'talking to herself', and 'told I was silly to indulge in imagination'. In time, some of the creatures in her private world became less pleasant.

Music meant a great deal to Deborah, and she desperately longed to learn to play the piano but was never allowed to. However,

> music featured prominently in my private world. It was the basis for fun. Music broke the coldness of the reality world. My imaginary friends often sat and listened to my singing and piano-playing. . . . I received trophies and other rewards for my perfect musical renderings.

Deborah believes her private world was a very important part of her childhood survival: 'I loved to be there . . . safe. I was nice. I wasn't the bad, wicked girl that the real world said I was. I felt important in my private world where my "friends" liked to hear me talking to them.' She belonged there: 'I felt it existed solely for me to find strength, in order to survive the world of reality . . . it was my outlet from the hells and pains of the real world.'

As an example, Deborah cites the time when, because she was so enthusiastic about music, she had been allowed to join the 'Sunbeam Group' of the local Salvation Army, but had soon lost her place for 'being naughty'. Alone in the garden shed,

> I entered my private world where, in front of a vast audience, I played the tambourine and curtsied to the applause. I especially remember this experience, because I 'saw' so many people, and the return to reality was such a sharp contrast.

Her private world was not, however, merely a wish-fulfilling day-dream. It included a 'Room of Judgement' in which Deborah was obliged, with exactitude and complete truthfulness, to justify her conduct before her imaginary friends. As the years passed, appearances in the Room of Judgement became more and more of an ordeal.

> During adolescence, when I so frequently found myself in the Judge-ment Room, going over and over some issue, looking at it from all

angles, I actually felt my friends didn't accept my version of events, and . . . I experienced real hurting pains on reflection.

The form of her private world changed over the years, in that 'the earlier simplicity gradually seemed to be affected by contradictions in the reality world'. And the Room of Judgement continued. Deborah was as a child constantly judged.

Deborah thinks her private world did help her, by alleviating her fears of people, 'to be accepting of different attitudes and personalities'; for there were often

times when I felt something akin to hatred for the guardians in my life who always seemed to be so confused and distant, and yet I was always left with a very guilty complex, as if *I* was bad to have these feelings.

Deborah could be used as a glib illustration of psychological theories of the imagination. Freud certainly would approve. An orphan, sent scurrying from one foster parent to another, dumped with a super-religious couple, has to find some kind of escape. Her fantasy world becomes her lifeline. There, she isn't judged, isn't bad, isn't condemned. Curiously there don't seem to be the figures you would most expect to find there – real parents. The guardians may be father and mother figures but they are not quite parental. And though Deborah didn't see it that way or explain it that way to herself, it's possible to see her Room of Judgement as a place where she tried to take control of her own life rather than letting oppressive adults make the rules and judgements.

CONCLUSION

WHY PLAY THIS GAME?

In the introduction I suggested that the information which Silvey and MacKeith collected was very valuable, because psychologists have tended not to look in much depth at what children produce in play. The temptation is, of course, to make rather grand claims on the basis of what are very limited data. There were only fifty-seven people who replied to Silvey and MacKeith's 'trawls'; most of those were drawing on memories of a long-gone past. The questionnaire they were asked to fill in asked them to describe not only their worlds but also themselves. Not surprisingly, forty of them said they were 'imaginative' and most said they were 'bright'. Twenty-three agreed that they were dreamy and an equal number said they were 'bad at games'. Does not playing football encourage playing more cerebral games? Discuss.

Despite the limitations, some interesting points do emerge. Apart from Deborah, none of these 'players' described a truly harrowing childhood. Some had problems like Rosalind, who lost her mother, or Holly, who hated moving to the country, or Jim, who was so cramped for space that he could be alone only in the privy. But for the most part, these worlds do not seem to have offered escapes from atrocious childhoods.

Children needed a measure of comfort and leisure to develop these worlds. Silvey and MacKeith were surprised when they discovered that, often, these were not solitary games. Children shared their worlds either with brothers or sisters or, sometimes, with friends. Occasionally a younger brother or sister would inherit the world when the older one grew out of it. Research would make one expect that most of those who devised such worlds would be first-born or only children. The literature suggests powerfully that such children are the most creative. In fact, the sample offers no proof of this at all. The 'paracosm' does not fall into this pattern.

Explaining why they devised such worlds was not something most of those who replied were clear about. Years later, could they really know? Their explanations sound as if the topic made them almost uncomfortable. Why spoil a nice fancy by being too searching? Some mentioned escape but others just spoke of 'great joy' or the pleasure of being in control. Others said they liked 'the act of creation'. This answer seems a bit odd: I wonder how many had heard of Koestler's book *The Act of Creation* (1964), which was fashionable in the 1970s, and parroted the phrase. Psychologists always look for 'deeper' explanations and, ever since Freud, play has not been allowed to be play. Children play either to develop motor skills or to master tricky situations or, the latest theory, because fantasy is healthy. Yet many of the worlds suggest that, having created them, the children perpetuated them as a vehicle for their latest hobby. If Jeremy was interested in languages, the main feature of Ktu became its language. If Godfrey was fascinated by medals and heraldic emblems, these became the dominant theme of his land. The imaginary world becomes a place in which to play hobbies which might not be that much fun to play elsewhere, or be allowed. It could be said that this idea confirms only that children play in order to master their environment but this seems, not just a drab way of putting it, but slightly wrong. These children designed their world to fit things which they were already interested in. It became a play space as well as an escape space.

The sixty-four paracosms collected by Silvey and MacKeith reveal two interesting patterns. First, paracosms can start very young – as young as 3. Most (72 per cent of the full sample) began between the ages of 7 and 12. Only a very few started after the age of 13. Imagination seems to be something that needs to start young. But children did develop more complex worlds as they grew older, either by elaborating their initial creation or sometimes by scrapping one fantasy as too childish and starting a more mature one. In the comments made on each of the children's 'fantasies', I suggested how very often the imaginative world was literal, paralleling with some variations the events of the real world. Real flights of fancy, such as Paul's Egyptian worlds with their Goon-like pharaohs, were exceptions. The paracosms are very much affected by the child's growing intelligence. The child may move from a world based on teddies and dolls to one based on politics, engineering, and newspapers. In one way, that reflects progress. The child gets more skilled at absorbing material from the real world into the play world. In other ways, though, this sophistication also means that often these worlds don't become any more imaginative with age. They are still very dependent on mimicking the real world; only the child's grasp of that world has 'improved'. There are grandiose exceptions, of course, like Denis's global railway or the benevolent socialist state, Possumbul, where a 'real' model is transformed. But one rarely sees explosions into creativity which may explain why, really, few of these children grew into successful artists despite the fact that they obviously loved playing with their imaginations. In Appendix Two, MacKeith offers an outline of the stages of development. It is a useful codification of material covered both here and in the play literature.

The other interesting pattern is one of sex differences. Far more than girls, boys tend to create these rather literal worlds: railway systems that owe a good deal to the Great Western Railway or countries that are Britain or Ruritania writ new. Only about one in ten of the boys' worlds emphasized dramas between the various characters who peopled them. As fantasies go, they tended to be rather impersonal. The girls produced more personal fantasies but, even so, few spun romantic worlds. Miriam and Margaret created almost the only 'Mills & Boon' universe, where languid heroines waited for gorgeous soldiers while pert maids flirted with the stable lads. The sexes were, in some ways, predictably different, though it must be remembered that these were mainly fantasies produced twenty to thirty years ago.

The question of why we play and why, as a species, we have developed the imagination has puzzled psychologists and philosophers for a very long time. These fantasy 'worlds' suggest that, for some children, the motivation to get away from the real world is very strong and persists into adult life. We don't really understand why but, if nothing else, these 'paracosms' show how strong the drive to play and imagine can be. When psychologists develop a proper understanding of play and the imagination, evidence like this will be very important because, if nothing else, these worlds show that playing isn't a frivolous and transient activity we have to grow out of by the age of 12 or 13. It might even be that if we learned to carry on playing, we might benefit as a species. Almost every other skill children learn is one they use as adults. Why not with play? Not that we can answer them now, but there seem to be two key questions. Why do we start playing? And why do we stop? One feeling that often comes through reading the answers people sent in was how much they had enjoyed the freedom to play as children and how, as mature adults, they often regretted the fact that they felt they couldn't do it any more.

CHILDREN'S IMAGININGS: THE NEGLECTED ASPECT OF DEVELOPMENT

Appendix one

A DESCRIPTIVE CLASSIFICATION, BY CONTENT, OF THE MAIN IMAGINARY ACTIVITIES OF CHILDREN AND YOUNG PEOPLE

1 Simple creative behaviours

A Transmutatory

The child pretends that an inanimate is another and quite different kind of object.

B Animistic

The child endows a thing with life, turning it into a person. (The age ranges involved differ considerably, for natural phenomena and for plants and animals respectively. See Buhler 1937.)

C Inventing people

(i) *Imaginary conversations* This is often not with a proper imaginary companion, but with a variety of characters in turn.

(ii) *Imaginary companions* The child invents, and continually relates to, an imaginary friend, who may be human, animal, or other.

2 Personally acting a part

A Being a machine

For example a motor car.

B Being a (non-human) living thing

For example a dog. During the 7–12 age-period, this, in many children, tends to merge into an intense empathy with living things.

C Being another (and particular) person

This involves taking over the role of, say, a baby, or an admired adult.

D Enacting an incident

Enacting, for instance, a family ceremony; or a school class; or a church service; or a journey; or a battle. Between, say, 7 and 9, the child is apt to display simultaneous vigorous physical activity. Moreover, at the same ages and even up to 10 and 11, there may be a tendency to form secret societies, and to invent vague and mysterious rituals.

3 Imagined participation in the action of the stories of others

A Hearing a story

This obviously includes listening to a story read aloud or told extempore at home, or told on the radio or television, or heard at the cinema or theatre.

B Reading a story (to oneself)

(As soon as the child is able to.)

C Producing a play with a standard plot

For example *Cinderella* or *Punch and Judy*, using a model theatre.

4 Invented stories

A Free-floating day-dreams

Either by day or before sleep, these reveries are spontaneous, uncontrolled, and ephemeral. Theodate L. Smith (1980) differentiated between the day-dreams of early childhood; 7–8; 8–10 (distinguishing between boys and girls); and from 10 to pre-adolescence. Jersild, Markey, and Jersild (1933) delineated rather similar age-ranges. They listed thirty-one varieties of day-dream topic! Elizabeth Hurlock (1950) described the special qualities of pre-adolescent day-dreams.

B Pre-sleep serial stories

This term applies when a story is continued from one evening to the next, usually for oneself, but sometimes for a younger sibling who is in bed nearby.

C Daytime structured short stories and dramas

Usually these are told silently by the child to himself or herself, but occasionally they are shared with one or more friends. Sometimes they are written down. Some children, boys or girls and usually between 8 and 11, invent the so-called 'Foster-child Fantasy'.

D Paracosms

These are spontaneously created imaginary private worlds, which for a considerable period recur in the child or young person, and therefore tend to become elaborate and systematized. They are much less common than, say, imaginary companions. Friedrich Nietzsche, the philosopher, had a childhood paracosm, as did W.H. Auden, the poet, Claes Oldenbourg, the Swedish-American artist, and various authors, such as Thomas de Quincey, Anthony Trollope, Robert Louis Stevenson, and C.S. Lewis. (See references in Silvey and MacKeith 1988.)

Appendix two

DEVELOPMENTAL SCHEMA OF CHILDREN'S IMAGININGS

Type of imaginative activity	*3–6 years*	*7–12 years*	*13–18 years*
1 *Simple creative behaviours*			
A Transmutatory	Quite common at 3 but lapses by 4.5	'Transmutation of place' sometimes occurs	Has lapsed
B Animistic	Common in many different forms	May persist for dolls, toy soldiers, etc. and for plants, animals, etc.	Has largely lapsed
C Inventing people			
(i) Imaginary conversations	Common at 3 or 4	Occasionally may persist, but privately	Very uncommon; quite secret
(ii) Imaginary companions	Very common; more vivid than ordinary day-dreams	Very much less common, except in boys 7–9	Uncommon
2 *Personally acting a part*			
A Being a machine	Common early in this period	Rare	Has lapsed
B Being a living thing	Quite common	Lapses, or changes, during this period	Has lapsed
C Being another person	Usually ephemeral, but sometimes obsessive	Sometimes solitary, but often in a group	Uncommon
D Enacting an incident	Very common; as an individual, or with peers or older sibs	Quite common; often done with peers or with sibs; 7–9 ...	Only in party games and formal drama

3	*Imagined participation in the action of the stories or others*			
A	Hearing a story	Very common; from parent, older sib, radio, and TV	Very common; from parent, radio, TV, and cinema	Very common; from radio, TV, cinema, and theatre
B	Reading a story	Reading only beginning	Amount varies widely	In some, almost addictive
C	Producing a play with a standard plot	With puppets, toy soldiers, etc.	Sometimes with own model theatre	Uncommon
4	*Invented stories*			
A	Free-floating day-dreams by day or before sleep	Common; are usually about play, sweets, riches, etc; before sleep, often spoken aloud in a muddled monologue	Fairly common, silent; Smith (1904) and Jersild et al. (1933) describe three age-stages of content	Very common, especially in girls; normally silent
B	Pre-sleep serial stories	Not very common; sometimes spoken aloud	Common; normally silent, unless shared	Common, silent; content now much changed
C	Day-time structured stories	Not very common, but sometimes shared with older sibs	Common, but less so than day-dreams; often written down; sometimes secret societies	Less frequent after 15; still sometimes written down
D	Paracosms	Uncommon; usually simple in form (19 per cent of our cases began in this age-period, usually at 5 or 6)	Uncommon; tend to become elaborate (74 per cent of our cases began in this age-period; the ninth year is the peak year)	Very uncommon (only 7 per cent of our cases began in this age-period; but also some persist from the 7-12 period)

FURTHER READING

Ames, L.B. and Learned, J. (1946) 'Imaginary companions and related phenomena', *Journal of Genetic Psychology* 69: 147-67.

Andrews, E.G. (1930) 'The development of the imagination in the pre-school child', University of Iowa Studies, *Studies in Character* III, 4, 15 November.

Baron-Cohen, S. (1987) 'Autism and symbolic play', *British Journal of Developmental Psychology* 5: 139-48.

Buhler, C. (1937) *From Birth to Maturity*, London: Kegan Paul, Trench, Trubner (especially ch. VII).

Casey, E.S. (1976) *Imagining: A Phenomenological Study*, Bloomington, Ind. and London: Indiana University Press.

Chukovsky, K. (1968) *From Two to Five*, trans. and ed. M. Morton, Berkeley, Calif. and London: University of California Press, revised edn.

Farjeon, E. (1960) *A Nursery in the Nineties*, Oxford University Press.

Green, G.H. (1923) *The Daydream: A Study in Development*, University of London Press.

Griffiths, R. (1949) *A Study of Imagination in Early Childhood, and its Function in Mental Development*, London: Routledge & Kegan Paul. Originally published 1935.

Harding, D.W. (1975) 'The role of the onlooker', in (ed.) *Language in Education*, Open University Language and Learning Course, London and Boston, Mass: Routledge & Kegan Paul (ch. 32, especially pp. 243-4). Originally published in *Scrutiny* 6, 3: 247-58, Cambridge: Deighton Bell, 1937.

—— (1963) 'The hinterland of thought', in (ed.) *Experience in Words: Essays on Poetry*, London: Chatto & Windus (ch. 10, especially pp. 196-7).

112

Harre, R. (1986) 'The step to social constructivism', in M. Richards and P. Light (eds) *Children of Social Worlds: Development in a Social Context*, Cambridge: Polity Press (in association with Oxford: Basil Blackwell).

Hurlock, E.B. (1950) *Child Development*, New York: McGraw-Hill (ch. X).

Jersild, A.T. (1957) *The Psychology of Adolescence*, New York: Macmillan (ch. 6).

—— (1969) *Child Psychology*, Englewood Cliffs, NJ: Prentice-Hall, and London: Staple Press.

Klinger, E. (1971) *Structure and Functions of Fantasy*, New York and London: Wiley Interscience.

Leslie, A.M. (1987) 'Pretense and representation: the origins of "Theory of Mind" ', *Psychological Review* 94, 4: 412–26.

Lieberman, J.N. (1977) *Playfulness: Its Relationship to Imagination*, New York and London: Academic Press.

Matthews, G.B. (1980) *Philosophy and the Young Child*, Cambridge, Mass. and London: Harvard University Press.

Minuchin, P.P. (1977) *The Middle Years of Childhood*, Monterey, Calif: Brookes-Cole (especially pp. 37–44).

Newson, J. and Newson, E. (1970) *Four Years Old in an Urban Community*, Harmondsworth: Penguin (ch. 7).

—— (1976) *Seven Years Old in the Home Environment*, London: Allen & Unwin (ch. 5).

Opie, I. and Opie, P. (1970) *Children's Games in Street and Playground*, Oxford: Clarendon Press (ch. 12).

Pitcher, E.G. and Prelinger, E. (1963) *Children Tell Stories: An Analysis of Fantasy*, New York: International Universities Press.

Ribot, T. (1926) *Essai sur l'imagination créatrice*, Paris: Librairie Felix Alcan.

Sarbin, T.R. (1972) 'Imagining as muted role-taking: a historical-linguistic analysis', in P.W. Sheehan (ed.) *The Function and Nature of Imagery*, New York and London: Academic Press.

Shotter, J. (1976) 'The development of personal powers', in M.P.M. Richards (ed.) *The Integration of a Child in a Social World*, Cambridge University Press.

Singer, J.L. (1975) *The Inner World of Daydreaming*, London and New York: Harper & Row. Based on his *Daydreaming*, New York: Random House, 1966.

Singer, J.L. with Biblow, E., Freyberg, J.T., Gottlieb, S., and

Pulaski, M.A. (1973) *The Child's World of Make-Believe: Experimental Studies of Imaginative Play*, New York and London: Academic Press.

Smith, T.L. (1904) 'The psychology of day dreams', *American Journal of Psychology* XV, 4.

Steedman, C. (1982) *The Tidy House*, London: Virago Press.

Sully, J. (1896) *Studies in Childhood*, New York: D. Appleton (chs II, XI, and XII).

Sutherland, M.B. (1971) *Everyday Imagining and Education*, London: Routledge & Kegan Paul.

Tomkins, S.S. and Izard, C.E. (eds) (1965) *Affect, Cognition and Personality*, New York: Springer (especially S.S. Tomkins, p. vii).

Vygotsky, L.S. (1962) *Thought and Language*, Cambridge, Mass: MIT Press. Originally published in USSR, 1934.

REFERENCES

Bruner, J.S. (1977) 'Introduction', in B. Tizard, *The Biology of Play*, London: Spastics International Medical Publication.

Claxton, G. (1984) *Live and Learn*, London: Harper & Row.

Cohen, D. (1987) *The Development of Play*, Beckenham: Croom Helm.

Eissler, K.R. (1962) *Leonardo da Vinci, psychological notes on the enigma*, London: Hogarth Press.

Eliot, T.S. (1917) *Prufrock and Other Observations*, London: Faber & Faber.

—— (1935) *Murder in the Cathedral*, London: Faber & Faber.

—— (1969) *Complete Poems and Plays*, London: Faber & Faber.

Fein, G. (1984) 'The self-building potential of pretend play', in T. Yawkey and A. Pelligrini (eds) *Child's Play: Developmental and Applied*, London: Lawrence Erlbaum.

Flavell, J.H., Flavell, F.R., and Green, F.L. (1987) 'Young children's knowledge about the apparent-real and pretend-real distinctions', *Developmental Psychology* 23, 6: 816–22.

Freud, S. (1905) *Jokes and their Relation to the Unconscious*, Harmondsworth: Penguin.

—— (1910) *Leonardo*; translated by J. Strachey, London: Hogarth Press.

Freyberg, J.T. (1981) 'The rich rewards of make-believe', in R. Strom (ed.) *Growing through Play*, Monterey, Calif: Brookes-Cole.

Gardner, H. (1984) *Art, Brain and the Mind*, New York: Basic Books.

Garvey, C. (1982) *Play*, London: Fontana.

Getzels, J.W. and Jackson, P.W. (1962) *Creativity and Intelligence*, New York: Wiley.

Gosse, E. (1907) *Father and Son*, Harmondsworth: Penguin.

Gregory, R.L. (ed.) (1987) *Oxford Companion to the Mind*, Oxford University Press.

Guilford, J.P. (1957) 'Creative abilities in the arts', *Psychological Review* 64: 110–18.

Hudson, L. (1966) *Contrary Imaginations*, London: Cape.

—— (1987) 'Creativity', in R.L. Gregory (ed.) *Oxford Companion to the Mind*, Oxford University Press.

Hurlock, E.B. (1950) *Child Development*, New York: McGraw-Hill.

Jersild, A.T., Markey, F.V., and Jersild, C.L. (1933) 'Children's fears, dreams, wishes, daydreams, likes, dislikes, pleasant and unpleasant memories', *Child Development Monograph No. 12.*

Koestler, A. (1964) *The Act of Creation*, London: Hutchinson.

MacKeith, S. (1982) 'Paracosms and the development of fantasy in childhood', in *Imagination, Cognition and Personality* 2: 261–7.

McWhirter, L. (1987) 'Ulster: The Power of Psychology' in D. Cohen (ed.) Beckenham: Croom Helm.

Moyles, J.R. (1989) *Just Playing*, Milton Keynes: Open University Press.

Parsons, M.J. (1988) *How we Understand Art*, Cambridge University Press.

Piaget, J. (1952) *Play, Dreams and Imitation in Childhood*, London: Routledge & Kegan Paul.

Pillsbury, W.B. (1910) *Industrial Psychology*, New York: Scribners.

Roe, A. (1953) 'A comparative psychological study of eminent psychologists and anthropologists and a comparison with biological and physical scientists', *Genetic Psychology Monographs* 67, 352.

Silvey, R. (1977) 'But that was in another country', Letter to *Times Educational Supplement*, 13 May.

Silvey, R. and MacKeith, S. (1988) 'The paracosm: a special form of fantasy', in D.C. Morrison (ed.) *Organising Early Experience*, New York: Baywood Publishing.

Simonton, K. (1989) *Scientific Genius*, Cambridge University Press.

Singer, J.L. and Singer, D. (1977) 'The values of the imagination', in B. Sutton (ed.) *Play and Learning*, New York: Gardner Press.

Skinner, B .F. (1948) *Walden Two*, New York: Macmillan.

Smith, T.L. (1904) 'The psychology of day dreams', *American Journal of Psychology*, XV, 4.

Storr, A. (1972) *The Dynamics of Creation*, London: Deutsch.

Tower, R.B. and Singer, J.L. (1980) 'Imagination, interest and joy in early childhood', in P.E. McGhee and A.J. Chapman (eds) *Children's Humour*, Chichester: Wiley.

Warnock, M. (1980) *Imagination*, London: Blackwells.

Waterhouse, K. and Hall, W. (1960) *Billy Liar*, London: Michael Joseph.

Winnicott, D.W. (1964) *The Child, the Family and the Outside World*, Harmondsworth: Penguin.

Wittkower, R. and Wittkower, M. (1963) *Born under Saturn*, London: Weidenfeld & Nicolson.

Wolman, I. (1982) *Handbook of Developmental Psychology*, Englewood Cliffs, NJ: Prentice-Hall.

INDEX

Adam Bede 44
Adam's railway 77–9
Aesop 76
Alice's world 34
Ambrose's world 88–9
Animal-land 30–1
A Peep Behind the Scenes 76
Asimov, I. 2
Athletic News 80
Auden, W.H. 22
Awentishland 68–9

Bannister, D. 5
Bearland 62–5
Beryl's island 56–8
Blyton, E. 87
Borel, J. 22
Borges, J. 2
Brenda's world 98–9
Brontë, B. 2–4
Brontë, C. 2–4
Bruner, J. 16

Castenada, C. 2
Cat Kingdom 25–7
Celtamania 81
Chagall, M. 2
Claxton, G. 17
Cohen, D. 10
Coneland 47
Crab 50–1
Cwayland 90–2

Dadd, R. 5
Darwin, C. 58, 76
Deborah's world 99–101
Denis' railway 65–7, 104

Dickie's world 51–2
Dobid 82–4

Eliot, T.S. 9
Evans, D. 2

Fairyland 38–40
Fein, G. 10
Freud, S. 7, 15
Freyberg, J.T. 17
Friskyland 31–4

Gardner, H. 18
Garvey, C. 17
Gatska Sandon 86
Getzels, J.W. 6–7
Gosse, E. 8
Green, V.H.H. 76
Greyfriars 66, 79
Gulliver's Travels 80

Hall, W. 19
Henderson, A. 74
How Green was my Valley 99
Hudson, L. 5–6
Huxley, T.H. 76

Jackson, P.W. 6–7
Jane's world 53–6
Jim's theatre 42–4
Johns, W.E. 87
Jungle Book 56

Kipling, R. 56, 58
Kish, K. 81
Koestler, A. 103

118

Land of Counterpane, The, 54, 84
Laura's world 27–8
Le Guin, U. 2, 70
Leonora's game 40–1
Lessing, D. 2
Lorna Doone 43
Luftstaad 85–6

Makrimanztec 92–4
Masefield, J. 28
McDougalls 75
McWhirter, L. 18
Morris, W. 75–6
Moyles, 14, 17–18
Mrs-es 29–30

Nesbit, E. 58
New Hentian States 70–3
News from Nowhere 75
Norman's railway 79–80
Novello, I. 94

Oldenburg, C. 2

Parsons, M.J. 19
Petsville 24–5
Piaget, J. 15–16
Pilgrim's Progress 54
Pillsbury, W.B. 6
Possumbul 73–6, 104

Reed, T.B. 76
Riding School, 41–2
Rilke, R.M. 9
Roe, A. 9
Rull 68

Santafagasta 84
Silvey, R. 1, 11–14, 19, 22, 23, 70, 80, 95, 102
Simone's world 36–7
Simonton, K. 9
Singer, D. 17
Singer, J.L. 17
Skinner, B.F. 5
Stevenson, R.L. 54, 58, 84
Storr, A. 8
Swallows and Amazons 60

Thirkell, A. 34
Tolkien, J.R. 2, 70
Tower, R.B. 17

Urilla 58–61
Ustinov, P. 22

Verne, J. 76
Veronica's school, 46–7

Warnock, M. 4
Waterhouse, K. 19
Watson, J.B. 6
Wells, H.G. 58
Weltonia 81–2
Winnicott, D.W. 16–17
Wittkower, M. 7
Wittkower, R. 7
Wodehouse, P.G. 2, 34
Wolman, B. 4
World 1 96–7
World 2 96–7

Xaalic 85–6